THE **POWER** OF **CHARISMA**

THE POWER OF CHARISMA
HARNESSING THE C-FACTOR TO INSPIRE CHANGE

DAN STRUTZEL
and TRACI SHOBLOM

Published 2017 by Gildan Press
an imprint of Gildan Media LLC.
www.gildanmedia.com

Distributed through the Book Market by Hachette Book Group, USA

Copyright ©2017 by Dan Strutzel and Traci Shoblom

THE POWER OF CHARISMA. Copyright ©2017 by Dan Strutzel and Traci Shoblom. All rights reserved.

Printed in the United States of America. No part of this book may be used, reproduced or transmitted in any manner whatsoever, by any means (electronic, photocopying, recording, or otherwise), without the prior written permission of the author, except in the case of brief quotations embodied in critical articles and reviews. No liability is assumed with respect to the use of the information contained within. Although every precaution has been taken, the author assumes no liability for errors or omissions. Neither is any liability assumed for damages resulting from the use of the information contained herein.

FIRST EDITION 2017

Front Cover image: David Rheinhardt of Pyrographx

Interior design by Meghan Day Healey of Story Horse, LLC.

Library of Congress Cataloging-in-Publication Data is available upon request

ISBN: 978-1-469-03571-0

Manufactured in the United States of America by LSC Communications

10   9   8   7   6   5   4   3   2   1

Contents

Preface ix
Introduction xiii
The C-Factor Quiz xix

PART ONE
What is the C-Factor?

1 The C-Factor: You Know It When You See It 3

2 Charismatic Influence 13

3 The Charismatic Mind 23

4 Charismatic Behaviors 39

5 How to Become a Charismatic Communicator 53

PART TWO
Applying the C-Factor

6	The C-Factor: The Equation	67
7	The Charismatic Leader: Religious, Corporate, and Community Leaders	71
8	The Charismatic Professional: Doctors, Lawyers, and Other Professionals	79
9	The Charismatic Entrepreneur	89
10	The Charismatic Employee	97
11	The Charismatic Lover	103
12	The Charismatic Family	111
13	The Charismatic Change Agent	119
	Conclusion: The Charismatic Life	127
	The C-Factor Quiz Revisited	129
	The C-Factor Challenge: A Thirty-Day Program to Gain Charisma in Every Area of Life	135
	Index	171

THE **POWER** OF **CHARISMA**

Preface

I was having an off day. Nothing too major, just the regular "life" stuff. As a husband, father of two, and the vice-president of new product development for Nightingale-Conant, I had a lot on my plate. So on my way to work that day, I wasn't thinking too much about the fact that I was about to meet one of the biggest names in personal development. I was thinking about an argument I'd had with my teenage daughter that morning and the Chicago traffic I found myself stuck in.

But as I walked in the front door of the office, I could immediately sense a different energy. It's hard to describe, really. Everything looked the same. The receptionist was there, as usual. I walked by Vic Conant's office, and he was at his desk with a cup of coffee, on the phone. Our engineer and producer, Dave Kuenstle, was gathering his notes before we headed into the studio. But something felt different. He hadn't even arrived yet, but Mark Victor Hansen, coauthor of the *Chicken Soup for the Soul* series, was already having an effect on the energy of the office.

Reflecting back on that now, I realize that I was feeling the impact of charisma. Pretty much everyone agrees that Mark Victor Hansen is the epitome of a charismatic individual. But how remarkable that his personal charisma could affect the energy and mood of others even when he wasn't around!

It was then that I started to think about charisma and began to notice certain qualities in the people I worked with. Each one of them had charisma, but not always in the Tony Robbins kind of way. Some were quieter and more gentle, like Ken Blanchard or Marianne Williamson. Others possessed an "everyman" quality, like John Cummuta and Luanne Oakes. But whether someone was a Wayne Dyer or a Deepak Chopra, every single one of the successful people I worked with had some form of charisma.

For years, that stuck in my mind. How can something as powerful as charisma look so different on different people? Does *everyone* have charisma? If not, can you get it? That's where Traci Shoblom enters the story.

I first met Traci, my coauthor, in 2008. She had been writing the workbooks that went into our audio programs for years, and we had worked with many of the same people, but had never met in person. We were going to create a program from scratch, called the FlexBrain Method, and I flew to Los Angeles so that she and I could have a brainstorming session over dinner in Redondo Beach.

It was an instant friendship! You know the kind—where you meet someone and within five minutes it's as if you'd known them your whole life. We talked about FlexBrain, yes. But we also spent hours talking about success and sharing stories of working with so many of the world's most influential people. "Oh, that reminds me . . . when I worked with him, this one time . . ." The evening flew by with laughter and great food, and our collaborative partnership was cemented.

When *The FlexBrain Method* came to be, we both had already learned that the brain has the ability to change and grow throughout people's lives. In the back of my mind I kept thinking, "Charisma *has* to be something that can be learned." But the timing wasn't right to pursue it. Nightingale-Conant was busier than ever, and with my travel schedule and studio sessions, and a deeply personal loss, the topic of charisma was put on the back burner.

Years later, over another brainstorming session (in a loud Mexican restaurant with some margaritas and tacos), Traci and I were talking about the qualities that make someone rise to the top of their field. We were getting ready to create *The Top 2%*, and were looking at what makes someone a success. We didn't call it *charisma* at the time. We called it *rapport with others*, and it included many of the qualities that are now in this book. We didn't know it at the time, but the C-Factor had been conceived.

The Top 2% was a huge success and has taken on a life of its own. The print copy has been on sale for years now, and it has changed the lives of thousands of people.

Last summer, as I looked around at the political landscape, the business world, and at the apparent dichotomy between the "haves" and the "have-nots," I realized that the time was finally right to explore the power of charisma. Traci and I began asking some important questions. What is charisma? Can you have it and not know it? Can charisma be used for bad?

That's how *The Power of Charisma* was born. We are both incredibly excited at how this book turned out and at the potential it has to change lives. To change *your* life.

If there is one thing I have learned from all the authors I've worked with over the years, it's this: we do have the power to change the world around us. But it starts with changing ourselves. And the C-Factor is a great way to do just that.

Happy reading!

Dan Strutzel

Introduction

I Love Bacon

It was a strange way to open an interview. "Don't judge me, Tracey, but I love bacon! I love a good burger!" The interviewer was Gayle King, Oprah's best friend and coanchor of *CBS This Morning*. She was interviewing Tracey Stewart, wife of former television host Jon Stewart, on being vegan. Ever gracious, Tracey replied, "I love many people who love a good burger!" After a laugh, the interview continued.

Ending more than fifteen years as host of *The Daily Show*, comedian, actor, writer, director, and producer Jon Stewart and his wife, Tracey, have recently begun to convert their New Jersey farmhouse into a sanctuary for rescued animals. When asked if he'd always loved animals, the acerbic comedian joked, "I was *so* angry at animals, before I met my wife Tracey." Clearly he's gotten over it, as he now has four dogs, two pigs, three rabbits, two guinea pigs, and two fish. And their happy home is about to get a lot more crowded. The news of his passion for rescuing animals has gone viral, and a simple Google search for his name brings up articles, links, stories, and videos about animal welfare.

So how can someone who is most famous for slinging arrows at politicians manage to create such buzz for an important social cause? Through the power of charisma.

You don't have to be a celebrity to use the power of charisma. It can be sparked by tragedy, as it was for Candy Lightner.

It was a warm spring day in 1980, just a regular day in the lives of a regular family. But it was a day that would change the lives of that family, and then spark sweeping change across the country. Candy Lightner's teenage daughter Cari was walking home from having her softball team photo taken when she was hit and killed by a drunk driver. Faced with the horror of every parent's nightmare, Candy took the intensity of her grief and founded Mothers Against Drunk Driving, the nonprofit organization dedicated to bringing awareness about—and stopping—drunk and drugged driving. At the time of this writing, there is at least one MADD office in every state, as well as in each province in Canada. MADD has been instrumental in enacting sweeping reform and bringing awareness to an issue that affects millions of people. And it all came from one angry mother who used her grief and the power of charisma to get people to join her cause.

Why Study Charisma?

Almost everyone has something they are passionate about. It might be a subject as large as animal rescue or drunk driving, or something as personal as getting healthy food in the vending machine at work. But without the ability to actually effect change, things just stay the same.

In order to truly inspire change, we need to be able to effectively explain the problem, inspire people to join us, create a vision for the new reality, and then motivate people to take the actions that lead to the change. Inspiring change requires charisma—the ability to communicate a clear, inspirational message that captivates and motivates another person or group.

Emmy award–winning special effects artist John McConnell describes what it's like when actor Morgan Freeman enters a room. "You can just feel the energy in the room change. It's like the whole room becomes more—I don't know—elevated. Voices drop to a hush. Everyone turns to the door to see who just came in. It's almost as if God himself walked in the room."

Imagine having that kind of aura, where all you had to do was walk into a room and heads would turn and people would want to hear what you have to say. What could that do for your career? Your personal life? The issues and causes you feel most passionately about?

But most of us don't have a television show, the aura of celebrity, or the powerful emotional catalyst of a tragedy to unleash our passion. Most of us are just regular, everyday people. Can we, too, use the power of charisma to inspire change?

The answer is a resounding YES!

Charisma is a social skill, like listening, that can be learned. And once learned, it becomes the difference between being heard or ignored.

The Benefits of Charisma

Charisma can benefit virtually every area of your life. Charisma gets people to like you, to trust you, to want to join you. Whether you're the leader of a country, the leader of your Girl Scout troop, or a freelance artist all alone in your studio, charisma can help you get what you want.

Here's a scenario that illustrates this fact.

Barbara and Carol are both project managers for a small video production house. They each manage a team of writers, artists, animators, and clients to produce videos for the Internet. But each woman has a completely different style for getting things done.

Barbara is a classic micromanager. She'll delegate a task, only to repeatedly call, email, or text the person to see if they've done the task yet and to offer suggestions on how to do it best. She doesn't inspire people to want to achieve excellence for her; she makes them want to do the bare minimum to get the job done so that Barbara will get off their backs. She acts one way with the clients and a totally different way with her team.

Contrast that with Carol. Carol is just as communicative as Barbara is, but her personal charisma makes her team members *want* to do good work for her. They're more willing to put in late hours, work weekends, and do extra rounds of revision in order to make a great video. How does she do this? Not by telling them to do it, but by using the skills that you'll learn in this book to *inspire* them.

Developing charisma will make you more effective at work, at home, and with your friends, and will even help you to motivate and inspire yourself.

Who knows—you might even inspire Gayle King to give up bacon!

How This Book Is Arranged

The Power of Charisma is divided into two parts. The first part goes into the theory of charisma—what it is, the different assumptions people make about it, charismatic influence, the mind-body connection.

The second part goes into the application of charisma, or what we're calling the C-Factor. Whether you're a leader, a parent, an employee, a change agent, or a lover, you can use the C-Factor to develop authentic relationships that inspire change.

Also, throughout the first part of the book, you'll find exercises called "C-Sizes." These are brief things you can do to improve your C-Factor.

The C-Factor is a magnetic ability to communicate a clear, inspirational message that captivates and influences another person or group.

Are you ready to discover your C-Factor? Turn the page and take the C-Factor Quiz.

The C-Factor Quiz

It's time to see how charismatic you already are. For each of the questions, rate yourself on a scale from 1 to 10, with 10 meaning "This totally describes me," and with 1 meaning "This doesn't describe me at all."

1. When I set a goal, I can clearly imagine what it will be like when I've achieved it.

        1   2   3   4   5   6   7   8   9   10

2. I speak with conviction and passion.

        1   2   3   4   5   6   7   8   9   10

3. I'm comfortable asking other people to do things for me.

   1   2   3   4   5   6   7   8   9   10

4. When I walk into a room, I get an immediate sense of the mood of the room.

   1   2   3   4   5   6   7   8   9   10

5. When I'm on the phone with someone, it's evident right away how I am feeling.

   1   2   3   4   5   6   7   8   9   10

6. I wouldn't ask someone to take a risk that I'm not willing to take myself.

   1   2   3   4   5   6   7   8   9   10

7. When I meet someone, I make eye contact and smile genuinely.

   1   2   3   4   5   6   7   8   9   10

8. People tell me their problems and ask for my advice.

   1   2   3   4   5   6   7   8   9   10

9. I've been told that I am overconfident at times.

   1 2 3 4 5 6 7 8 9 10

10. I tell great stories.

    1 2 3 4 5 6 7 8 9 10

11. When someone is talking to me, they feel as if they are the only person in the room.

    1 2 3 4 5 6 7 8 9 10

12. People feel comfortable to be themselves around me.

    1 2 3 4 5 6 7 8 9 10

13. I enter a room with confident body language.

    1 2 3 4 5 6 7 8 9 10

14. I'm not afraid to make fun of and laugh at myself.

    1 2 3 4 5 6 7 8 9 10

15. I am comfortable with who I am.

    1 2 3 4 5 6 7 8 9 10

Scoring

To find your score, add together the numbers you chose for each question.

1. _____
2. _____
3. _____
4. _____
5. _____
6. _____
7. _____
8. _____
9. _____
10. _____
11. _____
12. _____
13. _____
14. _____
15. _____

Total: _____

Results

15–45: A BIT SHY

If you scored in this range, you probably tend to be socially introverted and a bit shy. But never fear: charisma is a learned skill. By the end of this book, you are sure to have moved up the scale a bit.

46–90: IT DEPENDS

You're shy at times, but when you want to, you are capable of opening up and interacting with others. It all depends on the situation. The tools and techniques you'll learn in this book will help you feel more confident in your charisma.

91–134: MOSTLY CONFIDENT

Most of the time, you feel a deep sense of confidence. You like yourself, and others do too. Sometimes you wish you could be more persuasive. Once you learn the C-Factor, you'll be able to be naturally charismatic.

135–150: MAGNETIC CHARM

You are one of those rare individuals who possess natural charisma. You light up a room when you walk in, and people tend to gravitate to you. You tell great stories and can laugh at yourself. But you check your ego at the door. True charisma isn't about what others think of you, but how you make them feel.

PART ONE
What Is the C-Factor?

1

The C-Factor: You Know It When You See It

It was a hot spring day in Palm Springs in 1967 when author Colleen Collins met the King of Rock 'n' Roll, Elvis Presley.* She'd just finished marching in a parade as part of her high school drill team. Suddenly one of her friends shrieked, "There's Elvis Presley!"

Colleen looked across the street and saw Elvis, along with two bodyguards, trying to get into a dentist's office. Surrounded by admirers, Elvis was politely signing autographs. As usual, he was a polite Southern gentleman. "Thank you, ma'am." "I sure appreciate that."

After a few minutes, he thanked everyone and turned

---

* Colleen Collins, "Remembering the King of Rock 'n' Roll: The Day I Met Elvis Presley," Aug. 16, 2015; http://thezenman.com/2015/08/the-day-i-met-elvis-presley-by-colleen-collins/; accessed Oct. 12, 2016.

to go inside the dentist's office. Without thinking, Colleen shouted through the crowd. "Please, Elvis, just one more!" To her shock, he looked straight at her and said, "OK. Just one more."

It was surreal. The crowds parted and he walked toward her, as if in slow motion. He smiled and said, "What would you like me to sign?" She realized that she had nothing, so she turned around and said, "Sign my back, please."

She meant the back of her shirt, but he lifted her hair and placed the pen on the back of her neck and started writing.

"You're too sweaty for me to sign your back," he teased.

"I meant my shirt," she said. "Sign the back of my shirt."

As he wrote he spelled out, "T-h-e b-a-c-k o-f m-y s-h-i-r-t" as though he were writing those exact words.

She turned around and said, "Is that what you wrote?"

And he gave Colleen his famous curled-lip grin and said, "No, honey, I wrote my name."

When you meet a charismatic person, you just somehow sense that they are different. The energy around them is different. They have a sort of presence that makes people notice them. Many have called it the "It Factor."

Let's do a quick word association. Close your eyes and think of the word *charisma*. What famous people pop into your head? Your answers probably depend on a few things, including your age, your interests, and where you live.

For example, celebrities like Marilyn Monroe, Elvis Presley, Paul Newman, and others would come to mind if you are over the age of fifty. Younger celebrities would include Julia Roberts, George Clooney, Oprah Winfrey, and Matthew McConaughey.

But charisma isn't only found in Hollywood. Politicians such as Bill Clinton, Barack Obama, John Kennedy, and Condoleezza Rice are notably charismatic. Athletes like Muhammad Ali, Joe Namath, Magic Johnson, and Peyton Manning have used charisma on and off the field.

Interestingly, you don't even have to like or respect a person to acknowledge that they are charismatic. Extreme examples of this include Adolf Hitler and cult leader Jim Jones. These are examples of people who used their charismatic qualities to influence people to do horrible things. But they were still charismatic.

The thing about charisma is that it's a seemingly unidentifiable quality: you just "know it when you see it."

Charisma can be defined as "a constellation of personal characteristics or qualities that allow an individual to influence others by affecting their feelings, opinions, or behaviors."* Outside the context of leadership, it can be defined as "a dramatic flair that involves the desire and ability to communicate emotions, and thereby inspire others."**

But if that were the case—that charisma is some undefinable quality that no one can explain—then you could stop reading right now. You'd already either have it or not.

---

* R.E. Riggio, "Charisma." In S.J. Lopez, ed., *Encyclopedia of Positive Psychology* (Oxford: Blackwell. 2009). Pages: 984–997

** H. Friedman, S.R. Riggio, and E.D.Casella, "Nonverbal Skill, Personal Charisma, and Initial Attraction," *Personality and Social Psychology Bulletin,* 14 (1988): 203–211.

Of course we don't believe that. The premise of this book is that charisma is not a personality trait that one is born with, but is instead a learnable skill. Good for you, right? Or maybe you're already charismatic, but don't even know it.

Can You Be Charismatic and Not Know It?

Think back to the C-Factor Quiz at the beginning of the book. If you didn't score as highly as you would have liked, maybe it's because you don't have a self-perception of being charismatic. In other words, the definitions we just gave for charisma had more to do with the person's *actual* impact—what others think about that person—and less to do with a person's awareness of their impact on others. To say it differently, a person can be seen as charismatic by others and yet not see himself or herself as charismatic. It's all about perspective.

For example, a humble person might be uncomfortable saying they are charismatic, while an arrogant person might easily believe themselves to be charismatic. Would Moses or Jesus have described himself as charismatic? Would their followers have described them as charismatic?

An overly arrogant or confident person might answer 10 on each item in the quiz, yet other people might see that person simply as a jerk. (Remember Jim Carrey's character Ace Ventura in the movie *Ace Ventura: Pet Detective*?)

The point is that a person's true level of charisma does not depend on that person's beliefs or perceptions about their level of charisma.

Not to worry: you'll have an opportunity to take the quiz again at the end of the book, and you will also be encouraged to have others fill it out for you.

Assumptions about Charisma

This brings up an interesting point. We've already established that a person can have charisma without feeling charismatic. Yet, before you read the passage above, you probably assumed that a person with charisma would see themselves as having it.

What other assumptions do we make about charisma? Like all assumptions, some are valid and some are not. It's important to look at these and see whether they are true. Here are some assumptions to question.

Assumption One:
Charismatic People Are Always Charismatic

Have you ever felt completely confident and in control of a situation? Maybe it was a job interview that went really well, or a talk you gave. It was a few moments where even you were impressed with your own level of charisma.

We don't tend to think of those isolated moments as meaning that we have charisma, though. Instead we tend to assume that charismatic people are always charismatic.

It's not so! Many people would see actress Cameron Diaz as a charismatic person. But when she brought her dog to veterinary surgeon Ed Leeds (a personal friend of Traci's), she was just a regular person. "She walked in wearing no makeup, and a baseball cap," he said. "If I didn't know she was famous, I'd never have guessed it. She's just this down-to-earth person who was more concerned that her dog get quality care than being a celebrity." Dr. Leeds had a similar experience with Vegas personalities Siegfried and Roy. "When I spayed their white tigers, they weren't the stage performers. They were just a couple of animal lovers at home, who happened to have an amazing zoo inside their house."

Assumption Two:
Charismatic People Are Always Extroverts

Another assumption that we tend to make is that charismatic people are outgoing "life of the party" types. Research actually contradicts that assumption. One only need look as far as Princess Diana, Mother Teresa, or the extreme case of Howard Hughes to see that one doesn't need to have an outgoing personality to influence others.

Dr. Lyman Porter (or "Port," as his friends called him) was a classic example of a charismatic introvert. In academic circles, he was a brilliant mind who helped establish the field of management research. His theories and models have been taught in colleges around the world for more than thirty years. But to meet Port, one would see a simple, quiet man who wore sweater vests and asked probing questions. His piercing blue eyes and gentle laugh evoked one's kind grandpa more than a man who influenced and inspired generations of students.

Assumption Three: Charisma Is Innate

This might be the most common of all assumptions about charisma. Most of us look at a person with charisma and think, "Wow, I wish I could be like that, but I guess they were just born that way." Again, not true! While some people are born with a personality that is naturally charming, we've noted that charisma is about the effect you have on others. You can be charming and charismatic, or charming and sociopathic.

Charisma is a set of specific behaviors that affect other people. And if it's behavioral, then it can be learned. In an article in the *Academy of Management Journal*, researchers taught participants how to be more charismatic when giving a speech.*

An article in the *Harvard Business Review* identified a dozen "charismatic leadership tactics" or CLTs.** Nine of them are verbal: (1) metaphors, similes, and analogies; (2) stories and anecdotes; (3) contrasts; (4) rhetorical questions; (5) three-part lists; (6) expressions of moral conviction; (7) reflections of the group's sentiments; (8) the setting of high goals; and (9) conveying confidence that these goals can be achieved. Three tactics are nonverbal: animated voice, facial expressions, and gestures. Reading through this list,

---

* John Antonakis, Marika Fenley, and Sue Liechti, "Can Charisma Be Taught? Tests of Two Interventions," *Academy of Management Learning and Education*, vol. 10, no. 3 (Sept. 2011): 374–96.

** John Antonakis, Marika Fenley, and Sue Liechti, "Learning Charisma," *Harvard Business Review,* June 2012, https://hbr.org/2012/06/learning-charisma-2; accessed Oct. 12, 2016.

it becomes clear that these are techniques that practically anyone can learn. We'll get into more detail about charismatic behaviors in chapter three.

Assumption Four:
There Is Only One Style of Charisma

In our discussion of charismatic introverts, we have already pretty much blown this assumption out of the water. In fact, in her best-selling book *The Charisma Myth*, author Olivia Fox Cabane identifies four different styles of charisma. They are: *focus charisma, visionary charisma, kindness charisma*, and *authority charisma*.

Let's look a little more deeply at each.

Focus charisma is characterized by presence. People with this kind of charisma give you the feeling that they are fully present and listening to what you say. It's the kind of charisma seen in business with leaders such as Bill Gates and Elon Musk. Dr. Lyman Porter was also an example of focus charisma.

Visionary charisma is characterized by belief. People with this kind of charisma make others feel inspired. They make us believe! Think Tony Robbins or Joel Osteen. These individuals give others a sense of empowerment and belief in a better future. It's about projecting complete conviction about a cause.

Kindness charisma is characterized by warmth. People with this kind of charisma radiate total and complete acceptance of others. The Dalai Lama is a great example. People with kindness charisma have the ability to make people feel completely respected and accepted, often for the first time in their lives.

Authority charisma is characterized by status. It's the perception of power. This is often perceived by clothing (think of a doctor's coat) or possessions (an expensive car or home). It's also conveyed by body language—a gait or strut of confidence. Barack Obama is an example of someone with authority charisma. This is the kind of charisma that is the easiest to fake. We'll get more into the dark side of charisma in chapter two.

C-Size: The Power of Focus

All right, it's time for our first C-Size exercise. One thing we learned in this chapter is that people with the C-Factor are able to really be present and focus. So our first C-Size is to practice focus.

Set a timer for two minutes. Make sure that you won't be disturbed, so put your phone on silent, mute the computer, and lock the door. You don't have to lie down or sit in some lotus position. Just sit where you are, and focus on the present environment around you. First, what do you see? What does the room look like? Is it messy or neat? What is the decor like? Just take a few moments and look around the room as if you had never seen it before.

Next, what do you hear? Go beyond the obvious sounds and listen further. Do you hear a dog barking? Birds chirping? Traffic going by? Maybe you can hear a computer whirring or someone talking in the distance. Close your eyes for a moment if it helps, but just focus on what you can hear.

How about smell? Does the room have a particular smell? Can you smell your coffee or the air freshener?

Taste. Is there a taste in your mouth right now? Maybe it's the taco you had for lunch, or your toothpaste. Maybe there is no taste in your mouth.

Now scan your body for how it feels. Become aware of the sensation of your body on the chair and of your feet on the floor. What position are your legs and arms? Is there an area of tightness? Heaviness? Lightness? Does anything hurt? Does anything feel good?

By now your timer should be going off to indicate the end of the exercise. Practice this focus exercise every day for at least two minutes, and you'll be able to develop the C-Factor skill of focus and presence.

Now that we've looked at what charisma is (and what it isn't!), and have determined that charisma is more about the influence one has on others than anything innate to the person, let's take a closer look at charismatic influence.

2

Charismatic Influence

It's 10:00 a.m. on Saturday, and Justin Rudd is going to the beach. Not to sunbathe or walk his bulldog, POTUS. Instead, Justin is organizing the monthly beach cleanup put on by his nonprofit Community Action Team, or CAT for short.

With his shy smile and slow Southern drawl, Justin has influenced hundreds of volunteers to clean a stretch of beach in Long Beach, California, on the third Sunday of every month. Rain or shine, this team has conducted more than 200 consecutive cleanups, and Justin has been there for every one of them.

In addition to cleaning the beach, Justin and CAT host more than sixty charitable events every year. From food banks and clothing drives to father-daughter dances and a

Fourth of July bike ride, Long Beach citizens benefit from Justin's passionate commitment to giving back to his community.

How is one man able to garner such support from thousands of volunteers? Through his personal charisma. Justin doesn't give visionary speeches, but prefers to humbly serve with an attitude of grace. Justin's charisma comes from the way he inspires people to give their time and energy to causes he believes in.

The Power of Charisma

As we have discovered so far, the power of charisma lies in the effect it has on people. Harnessing this power can make a huge difference in your life.

If you're in sales, charisma can influence the way your prospects and customers treat you and deal with you. According to sales expert and personal development guru Brian Tracy, "Top salespeople seem to be far more successful than the average salespeople in getting along with their customers. They're always more welcome, more positively received and more trusted than the others. They sell more, and they sell more easily. They make a better living, and they build better lives. Salespeople with charisma get far more pleasure out of their work and suffer far less from stress and rejection. The charismatic salesperson is almost invariably a top performer in his field and enjoys all the rewards that go with superior sales."

He goes on to say, "When you have charisma, people will open doors for you and bring you opportunities that otherwise would not have been available to you. There is a close association between personal charisma and success in life. Probably 85% of your success and happiness will come from your interpersonal relationships and interactions with others. The more positively others respond to you, the easier it will be for you to get the things you want. In addition, members of your family and your friends will be far happier in your company, and you will have a greater influence on them, causing them to feel better about themselves and to do better at the important things in their lives."

The Norm of Reciprocity

In other words, when you have charisma, you're able to influence people to make their lives better. This leads to what is known as the *norm of reciprocity*, so the people you have helped then want to help you more.

In 1976, sociologists Phillip Kunz and Michael Woolcott used Christmas cards in an experiment to see just how many people would reciprocate the receipt of a holiday card by mailing their own Christmas cards back—to perfect strangers.*

Yes, you read that right. Perfect strangers. Kunz and Woolcott picked the names of 578 perfect strangers from the Chicago city directory and mailed them Christmas cards. Not everyone got the same exact card, mind you. Some people got expensive, high-quality cards decorated

---

* Melanie Tannenbaum, "I'll Show You My Christmas Card if You'll Show Me Yours," *Scientific American*, Jan. 2, 2015; http://blogs.scientificamerican.com/psysociety/i-8217-ll-show-you-my-holiday-card-if-you-show-me-yours/; accessed Oct. 7, 2016.

with poetry inscriptions and beautiful wintry scenes, while others got plain, white cards with "Merry Christmas" handwritten in red Sharpie marker across the front. Some people received their cards from "Dr. and Mrs. Kunz," while others simply received a card signed from "Phil and Joyce." But in every case, two facts remained: people received a card with a clearly marked return address, and that return address had the names of two people that they had never met before in their entire lives.

What would you do if you received a card from a perfect stranger? In this case, six of the strangers wrote back and directly asked Dr. Kunz for more information on how exactly they were acquainted. Another Chicago family with the last name Kunz actually reported that they had to call the police and complain about the number of people who had contacted them throughout the month of December, desperately seeking more information about who on earth Phil and Joyce were and how they could possibly know them. The experiment actually generated enough local buzz that it eventually ended when a local radio station outed the ploy, thus contaminating the reliability of any future responses.

But before that happened, 117 of the recipients—a full 20% of the original sample—had sent their own responses back to Kunz and Woolcott. These responses ranged from a simple mailing back of their own generic holiday cards to pictures of their children and pets to several-page-long letters detailing what had been going on in their lives over the past few years. Despite the fact that they had *never actually met Phillip Kunz before in their lives*, 20% of the recipients felt the need to respond to his Christmas card by sending their own cards back.

This study is often used to illustrate the norm of reciprocity: when people do something nice for you, you will likely feel *extremely* uncomfortable not returning the favor. If someone buys you a soda, you'll probably be more likely to buy some of the raffle tickets that he later tries to sell you. The Hare Krishna sect is intimately acquainted with this norm: it's why their members will hand you a flower in the airport before asking for a monetary contribution. So when you receive a holiday card—even if you don't quite know how you are acquainted with the sender—you will likely feel *very* pressured to reciprocate with a card of your own.

The Dark Side of Charisma

Thus far we have been talking about using the power of charisma to influence for good: visionary leaders who spur followers on to a better future; compassionate people who encourage acceptance and open-mindedness. These are people who use charisma as a force for positive change.

But as we have also mentioned, there can be a dark side to charisma. Some people have egos with such an inflated sense of importance that they use the skills associated with charisma for their own personal gain. It's charisma as an expression of narcissism.

In an article in *The Washington Post*, Joyce E.A. Russell describes the contrast between ethical charismatic leaders and unethical ones.

Ethical charismatic leaders will often focus on the organization's goals and build their message on common goals for all. They have noble intentions and will encourage and seek divergent views and foster open, two-way communication. They will be willing to hear feedback, even if it is negative about themselves and will accept criticism from others (rather than getting overly defensive). They will share a positive vision, helping their followers see the need for change and growth. Their focus is on building a more positive future for all, not just themselves.

On the other hand, the unethical charismatic leader will focus on their own personal goals and build their message based on themselves (even though it seems like they care about the masses of people). They will discourage and censor divergent opinions and will expect that communication should be one-way, (their way) or autocratic (top-down) communication. They will not be accepting of criticism and instead will strike back like bullies when they hear criticism (using the message that they "must defend themselves against attacks"). Their need for admiration and self-absorption can be so intense that it can lead them to believe they are infallible. Instead of painting an optimistic vision for the future, they will prey on people's fears and overly exaggerate the sense of crisis and pending doom (unless of course they are in charge). They are narcissistic leaders who can deceive and abuse their followers' rights. Using many superlatives (never, always, worst ever, disastrous, etc.) they inflate or overstate issues so that it seems like the "sky is falling."

This makes people feel like they need to follow them in order to be safe.

These leaders may take unnecessary risks, they may deny that problems or failures even occur, and followers have the tendency to over-rely on the leader for everything. They have unquestioning acceptance of the leader. In fact, sometimes people do not even know when they are being taken in—they can just be sucked up in the frenzy. Followers assume that everything the leader says is correct and they believe him/her. And when they finally realize that something is amiss or very wrong, they don't feel comfortable questioning the leader's decisions or voicing opposition or it becomes too dangerous for them to speak up.*

Blurred Lines

The line between ethical and unethical charisma is not always clear. Sometimes what starts out as ethical charisma slowly morphs into something darker. For example, charismatic leaders may use empowering language and popular buzzwords to create a sense of urgency in order to make things happen, but this technique can have negative consequences if a leader unfairly targets an opponent or catastrophizes events.** Another example is when a charismatic

---

* Joyce E.A. Russell, "Watch Out for the Dark Side of Charisma," *The Washington Post*, March 18, 2016; https://www.washingtonpost.com/news/capital-business/wp/2016/03/18/career-coach-watch-out-for-the-dark-side-of-charisma/; accessed Oct. 7, 2016.

** Kelley, R.E. (1988). In praise of followers. Harvard Business Review, 66, 142-148.

leader characterizes a vision as one that will "save" followers: "We need to take back our power!"* In those instances, followers can start thinking of their leader as their savior and as a result stop holding him or her accountable.

Using Charisma to Prevent Change

A person doesn't even need to be a corporate or political leader to use charisma as a force for bad. Traci, for example, has one friend who is always suggesting they go out to eat, even though Traci is trying to eat more healthfully (and stick to a budget!). These friends use their personal charm and charisma to influence you. "But it will be so great! Imagine sitting there on the deck, overlooking the lake. We'll have some wine and they have the *best* bread there. Come on . . . we can even get dessert. You only live once, right?" This person is not thinking about you or your figure or your budget. They want to have an experience and are trying to influence you so that they can have it.

Whether the unethical charismatic person is trying to effect a change that benefits him or her, or is trying to prevent a change that would harm him or her, it's easy to see how charisma can be used as a force for bad.

Remember that in chapter one we mentioned that authority charisma is the easiest kind of charisma to fake? It's because all a person needs to do is adopt the external trappings of charisma and they are more likely to gain the

---

* S. Baker, "Followership: The Theoretical Foundation of a Contemporary Construct," *Journal of Leadership and Organizational Studies*, 14 (2007): 50–60.

trust of followers. Go to the right school, drive the right car, live in the right neighborhood, belong to the right clubs, wear the right clothes, adopt the right speech patterns and body language for an ethically charismatic person, and most folks will believe you. But those things don't actually have anything to do with authentic charisma. Those are, in one sense, the disguise of charisma.

Authentic Charisma

What, then, is authentic charisma? It's the difference between the sleazy salesman who will use charm and the right words to convince you to buy a car you can't really afford and the salesperson who takes the time to listen to your needs and sells you the car that is best for those needs.

The key to being an authentic leader is in knowing oneself and leading by example, while the key to being a charismatic leader is in knowing one's followers and influencing them. Organizational behavior expert Afsaneh Nahavandi maintains that while authentic leaders do not need to be charismatic to be successful and that they can lead either by being task- or relationship-oriented, charismatic leaders necessarily have to have an "element of authenticity" to be effective.* So authentic charisma is the balance between knowing one's self, knowing one's followers, and keeping an open dialogue between the two.

---

* Afsaneh Nahavandi, *The Art and Science of Leadership*, 5th ed. (Upper Saddle River, N.J.: Prentice-Hall, 2009): 214.

C-Size: Social Media Reciprocity

OK, it's time for our next C-Size exercise. In this exercise, you'll do your own version of the Christmas card experiment, but through social media. Go to your favorite search engine and choose a few memes or short videos that convey a general positive message such as "Have a great day." Then go to your social media sites, like Facebook, Twitter, Instagram, Pinterest, Tumblr, even YouTube or Vine, and post the positive message. See how many responses you get. Do you get new friend requests and contacts? Watch the norm of reciprocity in effect!

In the first two chapters of part one, we've talked about charisma in a behavioral way, as something you *do*. In chapter three, we'll talk about the different mind-set of a person who has charisma.

3

The Charismatic Mind

The human mind is much like a farmer's land. The land gives the farmer a choice. He may plant in that land whatever he chooses. The land doesn't care what is planted. It's up to the farmer to make the decision. The mind, like the land, will return what you plant, but it doesn't care what you plant. If the farmer plants two seeds—one a seed of corn, the other nightshade, a deadly poison—waters and takes care of the land, what will happen?

Remember, the land doesn't care. It will return poison in just as wonderful abundance as it will corn. So up come the two plants—one corn, one poison. As it's written in the Bible (Galatians 6:7), "As ye sow, so shall ye reap."

The human mind is far more fertile, far more incredible and mysterious than the land, but it works the same way. It doesn't care what we plant . . . success . . . or failure. A concrete, worthwhile goal . . . or confusion, misunderstanding, fear, anxiety, and so on. But what we plant it must return to us. The problem is that our mind comes as standard equipment at birth. It's free. And things that are given to us for nothing, we place little value on. Things that we pay money for, we value.

The paradox is that exactly the reverse is true. Everything that's really worthwhile in life came to us free—our minds, our souls, our bodies, our hopes, our dreams, our ambitions, our intelligence, our love of family and children and friends and country. All these priceless possessions are free.

But the things that cost us money are actually very cheap and can be replaced at any time. A good man can be completely wiped out and make another fortune. He can do that several times. Even if our home burns down, we can rebuild it. But the things we got for nothing, we can never replace.

Our mind can do any kind of job we assign to it, but generally speaking, we use it for little jobs instead of big ones. So decide now. What is it you want? Plant your goal in your mind. It's the most important decision you'll ever make in your entire life.

—Earl Nightingale

These words were spoken in 1956, by Earl Nightingale, a charismatic leader and America's key motivational speaker. I had the honor of working with his company, Nightingale Conant, for most of my career, and Earl Nightingale (along with his partner Lloyd Conant) really influenced my thinking in many important ways.

Nightingale's record "The Strangest Secret" earned the first Gold Record for the spoken word. It sold more than a million copies. A million copies in 1956! It makes you wonder: how many of today's charismatic thought leaders were influenced—intentionally or unintentionally—by this so-called secret?

These days, it's not a secret that successful people use their minds differently from the rest of us. They tend to have greater powers of concentration and greater ability to focus, to see outside the lines of conventional thought. But where does that come from?

We posit that it comes from the mind and its companion, the physical brain. That's why this chapter is going to take a look at both. We know that charismatic people communicate differently. But do charismatic people *think* differently?

Decision Styles and Charisma

At the basis of most communication is a decision about how, what, and when to share information. Whether the information is considered good or bad, these decisions affect both how the information will be understood cognitively and how it will be understood emotionally.

Let's say you are a CEO, and your company is about to merge with another, larger company. You've got to tell your employees and shareholders this news. How are you going to tell them? What information will you share? These decisions will differ depending on how charismatic you are as a leader. And how you communicate this information will determine, in part, how it is received.

One particular framework for identifying decision styles is based upon a conceptual model originally developed by Michael J. Driver and then further defined by Driver and Kenneth Brousseau.* It's called the Driver Decision Style Model and explores how people make decisions through two dimensions—the amount of information they use when making decisions, and how many alternatives the person considers when making a decision.

Information Use

According to the model, people differ widely in the amount of information they use in decisionmaking. Some people reach conclusions on the basis of just a few facts. Others reach conclusions only after gathering and studying large amounts of information. Those who use low information to make decisions are called *satisficers*. The term *satisficing* means to use a few pieces of information to come up with a decision that is "good enough."

The opposite of satisficers are *maximizers*. These are the people who consider a *lot* of information before making a decision.

According to Driver and Brousseau, "Satisficers know that there is more information that they could take into consideration, but their tendency is to want to get on with things. They prefer to keep moving, rather than 'analyzing things to death.' At the other extreme is the maximizer

---

* Driver, Michael J., Kenneth R. Brousseau, and Phillip L. Hunsaker. *The dynamic decision maker: Five decision styles for executive and business success*. iUniverse, 1998.

mode. Maximizers want to be sure that they have considered all of the relevant facts, and that they have missed no important details, no matter how subtle. Their interest is in coming up with a high quality solution or in learning something new and important."

So in our CEO example, decision style is going to affect when and how much information is shared. A satisficer is not going to want to wait until all of the information about the merger is complete before talking to his people. He's more likely to have a meeting earlier on. "Many of you have heard rumors that we are going to be merging. Let me tell you what we know now."

A maximizer, on the other hand, is going to wait until he has all of the facts before talking about it. He'll wait until he can share the date of the merger, how many positions will be reduced, and what the projected financial impact will be.

Focus

As mentioned, the Driver Decision Styles Model also uses focus as one of its dimensions. People tend to fall on one or the other end of a spectrum when it comes to focus. There are *uni-focus* people, who are focused on generating one best solution, and there are *multi-focus* people, who tend to see different solutions or options as equally appealing. Driver and Brousseau say:

> Uni-focus decision-makers tend to have very strong views about how things ought to be done. Faced with

any situation, they usually have a very specific criterion in mind, such as cost, quality, or fairness, by which they will evaluate any potential solution. So, they usually will find a solution that stacks up best according to their criterion or goal.

Multi-focus thinkers, on the other hand, often use many criteria to evaluate potential solutions. They tend to have many goals. So, whereas one solution may fit some criteria very well, another course of action may fit other criteria better. Consequently, they are more open to alternatives and are more conditional in their thinking.

Going back to our CEO example, a uni-focus decision maker is going to be more likely to convey strong opinions based on a single criterion or goal. "We have decided to merge because it will help us keep the most jobs."

Multi-focus decisionmakers are more likely to give a longer talk, sharing *all* of the reasons why the merger is happening, for example: "There are five main outcomes we hope to achieve. They are increased profitability, greater flexibility in production times, the use of the other company's resources, access to technology that we don't currently have, and because it will help us keep the most jobs."

Four Primary Styles

So in this model, using both dimensions, we have four possible combinations.

Maximizer uni-focus. These people make careful and slow decisions based on a lot of information and analysis.

They want to find the best solution to the matter at hand. They are called *hierarchic*.

Maximizer multi-focus. These people use a lot of information and are happy to consider a lot of options. To them, decisionmaking is a process, not a singular event. They are called *integrative*.

Satisficer uni-focus. These use a minimum amount of information to quickly come to a clear decision about a course of action. They are called *decisive*.

Satisficer multi-focus. These people have very fluid thinking styles. Any piece of information will be seen as having different interpretations and implications. If the course of action they choose isn't working, they'll quickly move to another. They are called *flexible*.

In looking at this, we can see that people with charisma are more likely to be either *integrative* or *decisive*. A person who is *hierarchic* or *flexible* is less likely to be charismatic.

Role Style versus Operating Style

One other factor in the model affects the style a person demonstrates when making decisions and communicating. People tend to behave differently when they are in public than they do in their private lives. The decision process is different in front of a crowd than it is in front of a mirror. This distinction applies to all aspects of decisionmaking, whether the person is gathering information, evaluating or presenting options, or making a final choice.

When people are aware that they need to present a favorable image, such as in a job interview, giving a speech, or meeting the potential in-laws for the first time, they tend to behave in a manner that is appropriate for the role. The person behaves the way they think they should behave, not necessarily in their natural style.

But when a person is less self-aware of how he or she is thinking or behaving, the natural style comes out. This is the "real" person, not the one shown in public. This is why we said earlier that charismatic people aren't always charismatic. Cameron Diaz has the ability to be more or less charismatic, depending on whether she is in role style or operating style.

What does all of this mean for you? How can you use the Driver Decision Styles Model to become more charismatic? Remember that we've said that charisma is a set of learned behaviors that influence other people. So you can become more charismatic by adopting the decision style of integrative or decisive people, depending on whether the situation calls for role style or operating style.

To go back to our example, you're the CEO of a company that is about to merge with a larger company, but your natural operating style is flexible. This means that when you're in private, you'll use lots of information to come to a decision quickly. Your thinking about the merger is fluid as you're gathering information. But to convey charisma, you're going to need to present the information differently when you are making the announcement. If you share your thought processes, you could come across as wishy-washy or indecisive: "At first we were considering this, but then we got this new information, and now we are going to do this." Instead, you'll want to adopt the communication style of one who is either integrative or decisive.

An *integrative* CEO is going to have *visionary charisma*. They'll be the one who'll stand up there and share a compelling vision about how great things will be once the merge happens. They'll tell stories and get people emotionally excited about the impending change.

A *decisive* CEO is going to use *authority charisma*. He or she will get up there with the trappings of power, such as standing behind a podium with the company logo on it, surrounded by the top executives in the company. Sentences are likely to be brief and factual. "As you may have heard, we are going to be merging. After many months of talks and negotiations, both organizations have worked out a plan that is going to improve conditions for everyone involved." This is the CEO who will take a few questions about the issue, will tell everyone that a statement will be issued with more information, and then will leave the meeting.

So far in this chapter, we've talked about how charismatic people have different decision styles than those who aren't as charismatic. But it seems like a lot of work to have to force yourself to think differently in order to become more charismatic. Is there a way to train your brain to do it naturally?

C-Size: Adrift at Sea

Before we answer this question, let's have another C-Size. This one is actually a group exercise and is a modification of a classic consensus building exercise called "Adrift at Sea." But instead of generating consensus, we are going to look at the ideas of charisma and decisionmaking styles. So get a few friends together (four to six is ideal), and imagine the following scenario.

You are adrift on a private yacht in the South Pacific. As a consequence of a fire of unknown origin, much of the yacht and its contents have been destroyed. The yacht is now slowly sinking. Your location is unclear because of the destruction of critical navigational equipment and because you and your crew were distracted trying to bring the fire under control. Your best estimate is that you are approximately 1000 miles south-southwest of the nearest land.

Below is a list of fifteen items that are intact and undamaged after the fire. In addition to these articles, you have a serviceable rubber life raft with oars. It is large enough to carry you, the crew, and all of the items listed below. The total contents of all survivors' pockets are a package of cigarettes, several books of matches, and five one-dollar bills.

Your task is to rank the fifteen items below in terms of their importance. Place the number 1 by the most important item, the number 2 next to the next most important item, and so on through number 15, the least important.

First, do this individually for each member of the group. Then have a discussion about why you ordered the items the way you did.

_____ Sextant

_____ Shaving mirror

_____ Five-gallon can of water

_____ Mosquito netting

_____ One case of U.S. Army C-rations

_____ Maps of the Pacific Ocean

_____ Seat cushion (approved flotation device)

_____ Two-gallon can of oil-gas mixture

_____ Small transistor radio

_____ Shark repellent

_____ Twenty square feet of opaque plastic

_____ One quart of 160-proof Puerto Rican rum

_____ Fifteen feet of nylon rope

_____ Two boxes of chocolate bars

_____ Fishing kit

According to the experts, the basic supplies needed when a person is stranded in mid-ocean are articles to attract attention and articles to aid survival until rescuers arrive. Articles for navigation are of little importance: even if a small life raft were capable of reaching land, it would be impossible to store enough food and water to subsist during that period of time. Therefore, of primary importance are the shaving mirror and the two-gallon can of oil-gas mixture. These items could be used for signaling air-sea rescue. Of secondary importance are items such as water and food, e.g., the case of Army C-rations.

A brief rationale is provided for the ranking of each item. These brief explanations obviously do not represent all of the potential uses for the specified items, but rather the primary importance of each.

1. Shaving mirror. Critical for signaling air-sea rescue.
2. Two-gallon can of oil-gas mixture. Critical for signaling. The oil-gas mixture will float on the water and could be ignited with a dollar bill and a match (obviously, outside the raft).
3. Five-gallon can of water. Necessary to replenish loss from perspiring, etc.
4. One case of U.S. Army C-rations. Provides basic food intake.
5. Twenty square feet of opaque plastic. Used to collect rainwater and provide shelter from the elements.
6. Two boxes of chocolate bars. A reserve food supply.
7. Fishing kit. Ranked lower than the candy bars because "a bird in the hand is worth two in the bush." There is no assurance that you will catch any fish.

8. Fifteen feet of nylon rope. May be used to lash equipment together to prevent it from falling overboard.
9. Floating seat cushion. If someone fell overboard, it could function as a life preserver.
10. Shark repellent. Obvious.
11. One quart of 160-proof Puerto Rican rum. Contains 80% alcohol—enough to use as a potential antiseptic for any injuries incurred. Of little value otherwise; will cause dehydration if ingested.
12. Small transistor radio. Of little value because there is no transmitter (unfortunately you are out of range of your favorite radio stations).
13. Maps of the Pacific Ocean. Worthless without additional navigational equipment. It does not really matter where you are, but where the rescuers are.
14. Mosquito netting. There are no mosquitoes in the mid–Pacific Ocean.
15. Sextant. Without tables and a chronometer, relatively useless.

The basic rationale for ranking signaling devices above life-sustaining items (food and water) is that without signaling devices, there is almost no chance of being spotted and rescued. Furthermore, most rescues occur during the first thirty-six hours, and one can survive without food and water during this period.

Now comes the most interesting part of the C-Size—how the exercise reflects decision style. Let's recall the different styles.

Maximizer uni-focus. People who make careful and slow decisions based on a lot of information and analysis. They want to find the best solution to the matter at hand. They are called *hierarchic*.

Maximizer multi-focus. These people are ones who use a lot of information and are happy to consider a lot of options. To them, decisionmaking is a process, not a singular event. They are called *integrative*.

Satisficer uni-focus. People who use a minimum amount of information to quickly come to a clear decision about a course of action. They are called *decisive*.

Satisficer multi-focus. These people have very fluid thinking styles. Any piece of information will be seen as having different interpretations and implications. If the course of action they choose isn't working, they'll quickly move to another. They are called *flexible*.

Who in your group demonstrated the following decision styles?

Hierarchic
Integrative
Decisive
Flexible

Who in the group was a charismatic leader? Let's remember the different charisma styles. Did one or more people demonstrate charisma?

Focus charisma is characterized by *presence*. People with this kind of charisma give you the feeling that they are fully present and listening to what you say.

Visionary charisma is characterized by *belief*. People with this kind of charisma make others feel inspired.

Kindness charisma is characterized by *warmth*. People with this kind of charisma radiate total and complete acceptance of others.

Authority charisma is characterized by *status*. It's the perception of power. This impression is often conveyed by clothing (think of a doctor's coat) or possessions (an expensive car or home).

This is a fun exercise that can help you see your own decision style and the style of others, and identify the decisionmaking techniques of people with charisma.

The Neuroscience of Charisma

Earlier in this chapter we asked the question, "Is there a way to train your brain to become more naturally charismatic?" There is.

Researchers using EEG technology (brainwave measurement) to examine neural activation have found that charismatic leaders use visioning in their interactions with others.* They noted that charismatic leaders also have neural circuits that are more *coherent* (i.e., different parts of their brain are more connected to each other) than are those of other types of leaders. In the research, Waldman and others show that this coherence occurs when the right and left halves of the brain are in greater coordination

---

* Waldman, David A., Pierre A. Balthazard, and Suzanne J. Peterson. "Leadership and neuroscience: Can we revolutionize the way that inspirational leaders are identified and developed?." *The Academy of Management Perspectives* 25, no. 1 (2011): 60-74.

(i.e., activated at the same time) than is the case with the same regions of the brain for other executives. They contend that increased coherence results in a more holistic and authentic charismatic leader—someone who walks the talk.

Thus the more we engage in behaviors that are associated with charisma, the more our brains will lay down neural circuitry to become more charismatic. In other words, when we think like someone with charisma, and behave like someone with charisma, we will naturally become more charismatic.

In the next chapter, we'll go into more detail about the specific behaviors that are associated with the C-Factor.

4

Charismatic Behaviors

It's June 11, 1997. It's game five of the NBA finals, and the Chicago Bulls have the chance to take the lead in the best-of-seven-game series against the Utah Jazz. The Bulls have won the first two games; the Jazz have won the second two games. If the Bulls don't win game five, they will go into game six down three to two in the series. But the Bulls have a secret weapon—their charismatic leader, Michael Jordan.

At 2 a.m., Jordan calls his personal trainer to his hotel room, where he is lying in the fetal position and sweating profusely. He hardly has the strength to sit up in bed. The trainer and doctors diagnose him with a stomach virus or food poisoning likely caused by a pizza ordered the night before. "Michael," they tell him, "there's no way you can play."

But you can't tell the man who is famous for the line "Just do it" that he can't do something. So despite his sickness, Jordan gets out of bed at 5:50, just in time for the 7 o'clock tip-off. He goes off to a dark room and lies there, eyes closed, focusing his mind and getting his head in the game.

NBA.com reporter Steve Aschburner wrote, "What I recall from my vantage point in the auxiliary media seating—at the top of the Delta Center's lower bowl—was that Jordan appeared loose, jangly, weak. His whole demeanor seemed a little fuzzy around the edges, his cuts not sharp and, even from that distance, a vacant sort of expression on his face. Only in close-ups, though, and mostly in replays could I see how glazed over his eyes were and how profusely he was sweating. Think Patrick Ewing. In a steam bath. After a 5K run. About to audition for 'Dancing with the Stars'—that's how badly it was pouring off Jordan."*

"Every dead ball you could see it on his face, how drained he was," said John Paxson, a former Jordan teammate working his first season as the Bulls' broadcast analyst. "Then when the play would start, he'd summon something from within."

But Jordan slowly began to make shots even though he lacked his usual speed. With forty-seven seconds left, Jor-

---

* http://www.nba.com/news/features/steve_aschburner/top-nba-finals-moments-michael-jordan-flu-game-in-game-5-chicago-bulls-utah-jazz-1997-finals/

dan made a game-tying free throw and then came out of nowhere to grab the rebound after missing the second foul shot.

With twenty-five seconds remaining, Michael Jordan nailed the winning shot, a three-pointer, to give the Bulls the lead for good in their 90–88 victory—ultimately setting the Bulls up to finish off Utah in six games. With only a few seconds remaining and the game's result safely in Chicago's favor, Jordan collapses into Scottie Pippen's arms, creating an iconic image that has come to symbolize the "Flu Game."

Afterward Jordan reflected, "That was probably the most difficult thing I've ever done. I almost played myself into passing out just to win a basketball game. If we had lost, I would have been devastated."

"I didn't want to give up," Jordan said. "No matter how sick I was, no matter how tired I was, no matter how low on energy I was. I felt an obligation to my teammates and the city of Chicago to go out and give that extra effort."

Michael Jordan is widely considered to be one of the most charismatic people of our generation. He combines incredible athletic talent with a boyish grin and steely determination to embody the C-Factor. This anecdote from his basketball career illustrates many of the points we've made about the C-Factor thus far.

What was it that made the Bulls win that day? This clearly wasn't Jordan's finest athletic performance. He didn't give a visionary locker room speech. The man could barely stand up. No, what spurred the team on to victory was the *influence* Jordan had on the team without ever saying a word. His commitment to them made them even more fiercely committed to him.

The Charismatic Body

What, then, are the behaviors that can convey charisma without a word being uttered?

The article "Learning Charisma" identifies three nonverbal cues—expressions of *voice, body,* and *face*—as keys to charisma.* They don't come naturally to everyone, however, and they are the most culturally sensitive tactics: what's perceived as too passionate in certain Asian contexts might be perceived as too muted in southern European ones. Nonetheless, these nonverbal cues are important to learn and practice, because they are easier for people to process than verbal cues. In fact, Olivia Fox Cabane says that nonverbal cues and modes of communication are hardwired into our brains more deeply than the more recent language-processing abilities, so they affect us more strongly. In other words, our minds will pick up on, and believe, nonverbal cues for charisma much faster than verbal ones. Looking at behavior is the way to tell authentic charisma from false charisma. Here are some nonverbal ways to convey charisma.

ANIMATED VOICE

People who are passionate vary the volume with which they speak—whispering at appropriate points or rising to

---

* John Antonakis, Marika Fenley, and Sue Liechti, "Learning Charisma," *Harvard Business Review,* June 2012, https://hbr.org/2012/06/learning-charisma-2; accessed Oct. 12, 2016.

a crescendo to hammer home a point. Emotion—sadness, happiness, excitement, surprise—must come through in the voice. Pauses are also important because they convey control. This means to lower the intonation of your voice at the end of your sentences (no Valley Girl talk) and pause for two seconds before you speak again.

FACIAL EXPRESSIONS

These help reinforce your message. Listeners need to see as well as hear your passion—especially when you're telling a story or reflecting their sentiments. So be sure to make eye contact (one of the most important tips for charisma), and get comfortable smiling, frowning, and laughing.

GESTURES

These are signals for your listeners. A fist can reinforce confidence, power, and certitude. Waving a hand, pointing, or pounding on a desk can help draw attention. Reducing the speed and rapidity of nodding conveys confidence and power.

But none of these are what caused Michael Jordan to charismatically inspire his team that day. Instead, he created what is called *emotional contagion*.

The term *emotional contagion* refers to the phenomenon of "catching" someone's mood.* A classic example of emotional contagion is when babies who hear other babies crying begin to cry themselves, without any rea-

---

* Elaine Hatfield, Richard L. Rapson, and Yen-Chi L. Le, "Emotional Contagion and Empathy." In Jean Decety and William Ickes, eds., *The Social Neuroscience of Empathy* (Cambridge, Mass.: MIT Press, 2009), 19–30.

son of their own. Most people have had the experience of developing a good or bad mood based upon the moods of the people around them. Walk into a room with angry, hostile people, and you are likely to pick up on those emotions. Similarly, walk into a party or celebration of some kind, and your mood is likely to be lifted.

So when Michael Jordan put his own personal needs aside and pushed himself beyond his physical limits, he was able to transmit those emotions to his team. Charismatic people are more "contagious" than others. This is what can cause them to be so influential to those around them.

Here are some more nonverbal ways to convey charisma, adapted from body language expert Joe Navarro, author of *What Every Body Is Saying*.

WALKING

When we're with a friend, we usually walk at the same pace. It's almost like a march, but it's very synchronous. It allows us to walk in harmony and synchrony, and it very much indicates how we feel about each other. When we're walking with someone who is of higher status than us—someone we respect a lot, maybe an elderly person or a boss—we immediately adjust our pace of walk to the higher-status person's. We don't even have to think about it; it's automatic. So to convey charisma, you be the one to set the pace of walking. That isn't to say you need to run ahead. In fact, slowing down can often be the way to convey that you're in charge.

SITTING

Crossing the legs (either standing or sitting) is usually a comfort display. We see it around people who genuinely like each other. In fact, we tend to cross our legs in such a way that we will be off balance toward the person we favor.

The minute there are strangers present and they are violating your space, or the very instant you see someone that you don't like or may be a threat to you, you will no longer cross your legs. Your brain kicks in and says, "Put both feet down, in case we need for you to escape."

So crossing the legs is a high-comfort display. We do it when we're comfortable, we do it when we're pensive, we do it when we're around people we enjoy, and it quickly goes away any time we're uncomfortable or in a strange circumstance, or there's a threat.

To convey charisma, adopt a confident posture when crossing your legs.

ARMS

There are two ways to convey charisma with your arms. The one you choose depends on the kind of charisma you are trying to convey. One is called *arms akimbo*, and it's when you stand with your arms at your hips, with your fists facing backwards. Think of an angry mother standing in a room, indicating "Hey. Knock that off." It conveys command presence, and is a great tool for conveying authority charisma.

The other thing you can do with your arms is to assume the same basic stance, but change the position of the hands so that, as they come to rest on your hips, the thumbs are forward and the fingers are facing back. That changes the impression—it makes you look inquisitive rather than intrusive. This is useful in conveying kindness charisma.

Crossing the arms can have both positive and negative connotations. To determine which it is, you have to look at the grip. When people are talking to each other and their arms are crossed, but they're gripping their arms very tightly, it usually indicates something very negative.

Otherwise, this gesture isn't necessarily negative. One can have one's arms crossed, leaning back on a chair, and be very relaxed. When we are surrounded by people in a social setting, we derive a certain amount of comfort by putting our hands across our chest.

To repeat: in order to convey charisma, you want to convey the impression that you are as comfortable as possible in your environment.

There is one position that seems to convey the message "Don't get too close." It's called the *regal position,* because you often see kings and queens using it. In the regal position, you put your arms behind your back and hold your fingers together in some way so that your arms seem to disappear behind your back. You can't see the hands. This is good for conveying authority charisma.

HANDS

Putting the thumb and the first two fingers together, like an "OK" sign, can indicate precision. This is good for conveying focus charisma.

We can talk about something expansive by using *jazz hands*, where we extend our fingers fully and they stretch, and we are transported to something different. This can be used to convey visionary charisma.

Or we can do something that's called *steepling*. Steepling is when we bring our fingertips together but don't allow our palms to touch, so that our fingers look like a church steeple. Steepling is in fact the most powerful gesture there is for showing confidence. It shows that we're very confident about what we're talking about. With steepling, you don't have to yell, you don't have to scream, you don't have to raise your voice. You don't have to make eye contact. You merely have to bring your fingertips together, thumbs together, fingers spread apart, hands spread out, fingers still touching, and it transmits to the person who's hearing the message that you're very confident about what you're saying. It's an effective means of conveying both focus charisma and authority charisma.

SHAKING HANDS

The most important idea here is to not read too much into handshakes. Handshaking behavior is primarily culturally derived. You'll be able to tell how a person learned to shake hands, but that's about it.

When shaking someone's hand, you want to establish comfort. Mirror the other person's handshake. Why? This person may come from a society where they have weak handshakes, or they may have very strong handshakes. You want to mirror that. This is the first time you're going to touch that person, so you want to be on as equal terms with them as possible. You don't need to draw any further inferences, other than that culturally, this individual comes from a similar or a dissimilar culture.

The one handshake you must never do is called the *politician's handshake*. That's where you give somebody your hand, they give you their hand, and then you cover that hand with your free hand. Don't ever do that. It's always negatively received.

Lastly, when you do shake hands, make sure you make good eye contact. Make sure that it doesn't take place for too long or too briefly, that it's just right, and that it's established nonverbally. And if, for whatever reason, you shake hands with someone and you don't like that handshake, whatever you do, do not grimace. That sends a negative signal to that person, and the person may not understand why. Maybe in his or her society, people simply drape their hands in front for a very light touch.

Don't ever hesitate to say, "Let's do that handshake over again." The handshake is often the first time that two humans touch each other. It is a significant event in the lives of any two people and has lasting effects.

Let's try a C-Size to discover the importance of the handshake.

C-Size: Shake My Hand
In this C-Size, you're going to practice your handshake. In the next twenty-four hours, find at least five people to shake

hands with. Make sure that you get a good mix of people. Choose some you know and some you don't. Choose people of different cultures, genders, and power status. Use the pointers you've learned in this chapter to practice your charismatic handshake.

THE EYEBROWS

When we first meet someone, we often feel the power of the eyes in revealing emotions. Imagine meeting someone and, as you go to shake their hand, his or her eyes remain fixed. Then you meet another person, and as you go to shake their hand, they look at you and arch their eyebrows in what's known as the *eyebrow flash*. This simple act, the arching of the eyebrows for a tenth of a second, can transform a relationship. It can make people feel extremely comfortable. Why? Because when we arch our eyebrows, we're defying gravity. And one way of showing excitement and true emotion is by defying gravity. By arching our eyebrows and flashing our eyes very quickly, we're saying, "I feel really positive about you." It's usually associated with a smile. This is a great way to convey kindness charisma.

EYES

One of the most effective ways for a person to establish charisma is through eye contact. Again, there are cultural norms about how much eye contact is acceptable. You don't want to be staring someone down. But a confident, eye-to-eye gaze is a great way to convey all types of charisma.

SMILING

The most important thing about your smile is that it be genuine. It's got to go all the way up to the eyes. The false smile—the social smile—is the smile that moves the corners of the mouth toward the ears, but does not involve the eyes. This is one way of assessing genuine emotions. The true smile involves the eyes; with the false smile there is no eye involvement. So if you can't smile genuinely, don't smile at all.

Let's go back to our CEO from the last chapter. He's got to tell his employees that they will be merging with another company, and he wants to convey charisma and influence them to believe that the merge is going to be a good thing. He's not trying to trick them—he really believes it's for the best. He just wants to convey this as effortlessly as possible. As we've learned in this chapter, the best way to do that is through body language.

As he's getting ready to walk out on stage, he stands tall and thinks of something that will make him feel genuinely happy and confident. He smiles and strides out to the podium. Without saying a word, he does the eyebrow raise at a couple of people and grins. He puts his hand on either side of the podium, with his thumbs toward the audience. That helps him to convey openness. He stands with one leg slightly crossed over the other, conveying comfort. He stops and looks at the audience for a couple of seconds before finally speaking. Slowly, and with a steady voice, he says, "Good morning."

We can see that, although our CEO has only said two words, his body language has conveyed confidence, comfort, and authority. This goes a long way to establishing the charisma he'll need to convey the message that the future will be better.

In this chapter, we've talked about the behaviors that are associated with charisma. But as we have been saying all along, charisma is something that is attributed to a person by others. So in the next chapter we'll take a look at the verbal cues that cause a person to be seen as charismatic. After all, it's not whether *you* think you have charisma. It's whether others see you that way.

5

How to Become a Charismatic Communicator

The woman waited off stage for her introduction to be complete. She had participated in a giving project and wanted to share her experiences, as well as to encourage the audience members to give back to their community.

As soon as she heard the applause after her name, she ascended the stairs to the stage. Instead of going behind the podium, she grabbed the microphone and walked to the very front of the stage. Holding the microphone up, she paused, looked around at the silent crowd, and began to speak.

"One day, a boy went fishing in a small boat with his dad. At some point, when they were in the middle of the lake, the boy starts chuckling. The dad says, 'What? Why are you laughing?' The dad looks down and is surprised to see that the boy has poked a hole in the bottom of the boat, and water is starting to flood it. As the dad is bailing out the boat with his hat, he says to the boy, 'Why on earth would you do that?' The boy is still laughing and says, 'Look at where the hole is! It's on *your* side of the boat!' He didn't understand that they were in the same boat together.

"I think that's how it is with people in need. We really are in the same boat together.

"This was an amazing week for me. I have to say that I learned almost as much from who *didn't* help me as from those who did. I was quite surprised at how challenging it was to get people to help me give away $1500 to others.

"I contacted ten people. I put the call out on Facebook, Twitter, and LinkedIn. I put the word out to all of those people, and I heard back from three. Three people.

"Are there really that many people who don't get that we're all in the same boat?

"I am grateful, though, for the three people who agreed to help me. With the help of these three people, I was able to help twenty-one people in need.

"Imagine that you're five years old. You come to school hungry most days. Your whole class is going on a field trip to pick and eat strawberries at a farm. But you can't go because your mom can't afford the $12 ticket. So every day you go to school and your classmates are talking about the trip that you can't go on. That was the case for ten kindergarten students at a local elementary school. You're *five years old*. But thanks to their teacher and this giving project, I was able to give the tickets to those students.

"Now imagine that you're in the eighth grade. You're on the honor roll and in the student council. But you have to walk three miles through one of our city's roughest neighborhoods to get to school and back. You're in the eighth grade—the prime age for boys to get involved with drugs and gangs and crime. You're trying to do the right thing. But it gets harder every day. Thanks to the giving project, I was able to buy this young man a bus pass that will last until the end of the school year.

"Next, imagine that you are a single mother. You've got three kids, and you're driving them around in an unsafe car because you can't afford the repairs. Your car keeps overheating, and you know it's dangerous. But what can you do? You need a car. Thanks to the kind folks at a local auto repair shop, and this giving project, I was able to pay for this young mother's auto repair.

"Finally, let's imagine the worst case scenario. We just had a bitter, wet, cold winter storm. Imagine that you're homeless. You're wet and cold and hungry. All you want is a blanket and some basic supplies for your human dignity. Thanks to the inspiration of the homeless shelter, I was able to make up five bags just like this one. It contains things like BandAids, ChapStick, a toothbrush, and toothpaste. I got them socks and mittens and a blanket. And other things that you and I take for granted.

"Before I go tonight, I want to remind everyone that we all are in the same boat. When one child is ashamed because she can't go on a field trip with her class, we should all be ashamed. When one young man is in danger because he has no transportation to school, we all are in danger.

When a young mother has to put her children at risk in an unsafe car, we are all at risk. When a homeless person doesn't even have a blanket on a cold winter night . . .

"It's just not right. If you get nothing else out of this evening, I hope you get the message that it doesn't take a lot to help another person in need. And by doing so, you're helping yourself. Because we really are all in the same boat."

As the audience stood clapping, the woman walked offstage with tears glistening in her eyes. Sure, some would call her talk charismatic. But all she cared about was whether or not it inspired others to make a difference.

We've mentioned throughout the book that charisma is a set of behaviors that cause others to be magnetically attracted to a person. We're calling that the C-Factor. We've explored the types of charisma and the mind-set that goes into developing charisma. We've looked at nonverbal elements. But when it comes down to it, charisma is about communication. It's about conveying a message—some message—in a way that changes the behaviors of the people around you.

As you recall, we said that the *Harvard Business Review* (HBR) identified a dozen charismatic leadership tactics or CLTs. Nine of them are verbal: *metaphors, similes, and analogies; stories and anecdotes; contrasts; rhetorical questions; three-part lists; expressions of moral conviction; reflections of the group's sentiments; the setting of high goals; and conveying confidence that they can be achieved*. The example given in the story illustrates several of these CLTs. The HBR article broke it down into three categories. They are "Connect,

Compare, and Contrast"; "Engage and Distill"; and "Show Integrity, Authority, and Passion." Let's walk through them one at a time.

Connect, Compare, and Contrast

Charismatic speakers help listeners understand, relate to, and remember a message. A powerful way to do this is by using *metaphors, similes,* and *analogies.* You remember from elementary school that a *metaphor* is a figure of speech in which a word or phrase is applied to an object or action to which it is not literally applicable. "I was floating on a cloud!" A *simile* is the same thing, but using the words "like" or "as." "I was as hungry as a bear." An *analogy* is a comparison between two things that are similar in a significant way. "Just as a caterpillar comes out of its cocoon, so we must come out of our comfort zone."

Using metaphors, similes, and analogies helps charismatic communicators make an instant connection with the audience in virtually any context. "When I heard that Joe had been fired, I felt as if I'd been punched in the stomach."

Stories and *anecdotes* also make messages more engaging and help listeners connect with the speaker. You don't have to be a professional speaker to make the most of this technique. You just have to tie the story to your point in an emotionally compelling way. "My daughter brought home a kitten last weekend that she had found abandoned in a rainy parking lot. She only heard the kitten because it was crying so loudly. Why, then, are we so easily able to ignore the cries of the unfortunate?"

Contrasts are a key CLT because they combine reason and passion; they clarify your position by pitting it against the opposite, often to dramatic effect. "I stand here, not as your boss, but as your friend."

Engage and Distill

The second category of CLT is Engage and Distill. This category encompasses *rhetorical questions* and *three-part lists*.

A *rhetorical question* is one that doesn't expect to receive an actual answer. It might even have an obvious answer. It is asked to get the audience thinking. You have asked the question to make a point, to persuade, or for literary effect. When the woman in our example above asked, "Are there really that many people who don't get that we're all in the same boat?", it was a rhetorical question.

Three-part lists are another old trick of effective persuasion, because they distill any message into key takeaways. Why three? According to the HBR article, "Because most people can remember three things; three is sufficient to provide proof of a pattern; and three gives an impression of completeness. Three-part lists can be announced—as in 'There are three things we need to do to get our bottom line back into the black'—or they can be under the radar, as in the sentence before this one."

The woman giving the speech used a three-part list, although she didn't number the parts. "Thanks to the inspiration of the homeless shelter, I was able to make up five bags just like this one. (1) It contains things like BandAids, ChapStick, a toothbrush, and toothpaste. (2) I got them socks and mittens and a blanket. (3) And other things that you and I take for granted."

Show Integrity, Authority, and Passion

The final category of CLTs is Integrity, Authority, and Passion. These correlate nicely to the types of charisma we've been talking about so far.

Expressions of moral conviction *and* statements that reflect the sentiments of the group—even when the sentiments are negative—establish your credibility by revealing the quality of your character to your listeners and making them identify and align themselves with you. In the talk, the woman did this by telling the audience that "we should all be ashamed."

Another CLT, which helps charismatic leaders demonstrate passion—and inspire it in their followers—is *setting high goals*. "We want to spark a political revolution!" Or "we want every child to have access to heathy food at home."

But one must also *convey confidence that the goals can be achieved*. Using a three-part list can help this. "I know that we have the talent. We have the drive. We just need the resources!"

C-Size: Communication Charisma

Now it's your turn. Prepare a talk using the CLTs. (It doesn't matter if you actually give the talk, although it's better practice if you do.) Incorporate the things you've learned thus far in this book: metaphors, similes, and analogies; stories and anecdotes; contrasts; rhetorical questions; three-part lists; expressions of moral conviction; reflections of the group's sentiments; the setting of high goals; and conveying confidence that they can be achieved. Be sure and practice the nonverbal CLTs as well: animated voice, facial expressions, and gestures.

Don't be afraid to use a little self-deprecating humor. Here is an example from a woman who'd given a talk and had a book signing in her hometown, and no one came. She now tells this anecdote as a way of connecting with her audience.

"Things look encouraging as I pull up. My name is all over the store. They have a table for me right in front. I *am* going to be the famous author returning. Won't my friends and family be proud?

"'Sign up for my raffle!' I enthusiastically say as shoppers enter the store. 'No, thank you.'

"'I wrote a book!' I say with a big smile.

"'Good for you.'

"'Want me to sign a copy for you?'

"'No, thank you.'

"My mood was plummeting. I've driven 900 miles to *not* give a talk and to have *not* signed any books. I could have done this at home.

"At the end of my two hours I packed it up.

"My poor father was hurting for me. He wanted so much to see me succeed. He said, 'How about you give us the talk, and we will use my professional video equipment to tape it?' He was a broadcaster for forty years and knows the business. 'At least your whole trip wouldn't be a waste.'

"So I scraped myself up off the floor, wiped my tears, put on some makeup and gave my talk to my parents, the video camera, and five chintz pillows. My sixteen-year-old niece would have been there, but we'd accidentally locked her in the backyard.

"The tape turned out really well. You couldn't see the tear stains on my cheeks, I didn't look as fat as I thought I would, and my dad really loved the talk. But then again, he already knows how to read."

Charisma in a Crisis

What are you like in a crisis? Are you the kind of person who keeps it together during the actual crisis but falls apart afterward? Or do stressful situations push you over the edge?

Research has shown that stressful situations tends to cause leaders to be perceived as being more charismatic than they were before.* Is this because the leader became more charismatic, or because the crisis brought out opportunities for the leader to demonstrate already-present charismatic traits? Actually, it's both. The crisis allows the leader to demonstrate more charisma—especially visionary charisma. The leader is more visible, and there are higher emotional stakes for the followers.

Crisis has been an inherent part of charismatic leadership since sociologist Max Weber's original concep-

---

* R. Mark Bell, "Charismatic Leadership Case Study with Ronald Reagan as Exemplar," *Emerging Leadership Journeys* 65, no. 1 (2013): 83–91.

tualization of charismatic authority back in 1947, and a great deal of research and theory has linked charisma to crisis. Some scholars have found that the number of crises faced by American presidents was related to ratings of their charisma. Sociologist J.A. Conger said, "Context is not the key determinant, but rather the leader and context influence one another—the relative weight of each influence varying from situation to situation." Another expert, Alan E. Bryman, suggests there are at least two reasons why charismatic leadership should be associated with crisis. The first is that a crisis provides charismatic leaders with the opportunity to display charismatic behavior. Scholar G.A. Yukl holds that the uncertainty and ambiguity of the situation itself contribute to an increase in the leader's ability to be charismatic. A problem gives the leader the opportunity to be innovative and to deviate from the status quo in creating a solution. Moreover, a tumultuous situation provides the leader with a cause for which he or she can build support from followers. For example, after the crisis of 9/11, President George W. Bush was seen as more charismatic than before because he used more charismatic language in his speeches. (This perception has changed over time, as more information has come to light about the events of that day.)

In addition, followers tend to become more attached to their leaders under times of stress. When situations are ambiguous, people tend to look to their leaders to provide reassurance, support, and direction.

As we've said before, charisma is important only to the extent that it influences others. So really, whether the crisis brings out charismatic behaviors or whether others just think it does is irrelevant.

In part one of *The C-Factor*, we've talked quite a bit about what charisma is and how to develop it. Up to this point, it's been mostly theoretical. In part two, we will begin to apply the ideas we've learned in order to develop charisma in several key roles that people find themselves in. But first we'll develop an equation for the C-Factor that represents what we've established about charisma that can be applied to each of these roles.

PART TWO
Applying the C-Factor

6

The C-Factor: The Equation

You'll remember from the beginning of the book that the C-Factor is a magnetic ability to communicate a clear, inspirational message that captivates and influences another person or group. It can be summed up by the following equation.

$$C = f(P_1 * P_2 * E_x)$$

Don't get freaked out by flashbacks of algebra class. The C-Factor can be expressed by the following sentence too. *Charisma is a function of the qualities of Person One times the qualities of Person Two, affected by The Environment.*

In part one of the book, we explained that there are certain qualities that a charismatic person has. There are verbal and nonverbal ways of communicating. A charismatic person has a different mind-set—and even different neural patterns—than a person without charisma. These are the qualities of P_1 or Person One.

We also mentioned that charisma is something that is attributed to you by another person. There's no such thing as charisma if you're alone in a forest talking to trees. Charisma is in the eye of the beholder. It's why a person can be charismatic and not know it. It's why your daughter might think that Justin Bieber is the most charismatic person that ever lived, and you don't see it at all.

This interaction can be represented by this figure, known as "The Johari Window," invented by psychologists Joseph Luft and Harrington Ingham.*

Charisma

	Known to self	Not known to self
Known to others	**OPEN**	**BLIND SPOT**
Not known to others	**HIDDEN**	**UNKNOWN**

---

* Luft, J. (1969). *Of Human Interaction*. Palo Alto, California: National Press.

In Quadrant One (Open), the person thinks they have charisma, and other people agree. This would be the typical scenario.

In Quadrant Two (Blind Spot), the person doesn't think they are all that charismatic, but other people do think of them as having charisma. This is the humble person—perhaps the introvert—who doesn't really know how much influence they have on others.

In Quadrant Three (Hidden), the person thinks they are charismatic, but others don't agree. This is the guy who thinks he is charming, even though people secretly hate him.

In Quadrant Four (Unknown), the person doesn't think of themselves as having charisma, and other people don't either.

For us, the most interesting quadrants are Two and Four, because that's where the C-Factor can be developed. We're not going to do much for the person who already has a lot of charisma, or the person who thinks he does but really doesn't. But for the person whom other people see as charismatic, even though they themselves don't, or for the person whom no one thinks is charismatic, there is room for growth.

There is another variable in our C-Factor equation, and that's The Environment. As we've already said, The Environment is a factor in whether or not a person will be charismatic. Cameron Diaz isn't charismatic 24/7. When she is at the vet, she is just a regular person with a dog. But when she's on the red carpet, she is charismatic. This is why you can have moments when you are totally charismatic and captivating, and others when you feel insecure and unsure.

The C-Factor, then, is a combination of the qualities of the person who is charismatic, the qualities of the other person, and the environment they are both in. Again:

$$C = f(P_1 * P_2 * E_x)$$

So if you are P_1, how can you use the C-Factor equation to become more charismatic? Whether you're an entrepreneur, a doctor, a lawyer, or a business executive, the way to stand out to the public is through projecting your personality in such a way that it connects with those you encounter on a deep and memorable level. Again, it's not about projecting an egotistic air of "Aren't I great?" It's about genuine, authentic communication.

There are five components of personal charisma that are easy for the average person to begin working on.* You'll recognize them from part one of this book.

1. Be self-confident.
2. Tell great stories.
3. Use body language.
4. Make the conversation about the person you're talking to.
5. Be a good listener.

In the next few chapters, we'll apply these concepts to the different roles people can have in their lives and show how you can increase your C-Factor.

---

* Denise Restauri, "Five Qualities of Charismatic People: How Many Do You Have?"; *Forbes*, May 12, 2012; http://www.forbes.com/sites/deniserestauri/2012/05/03/5-qualities-of-charismatic-people-how-many-do-you-have/#3a657e73372d; accessed Oct. 14, 2016.

7

The Charismatic Leader: Religious, Corporate, and Community Leaders

Passing on the opportunity to dine with politicians after addressing Congress in September 2015, Pope Francis instead said a prayer blessing a meal for homeless clients of St. Maria's Meals, a food program run by Catholic Charities in Washington, D.C.*

Just before the meal, Francis drew a powerful comparison between the plight of the homeless and the Christmas story about Jesus' birth in a stable.

"The son of God knew what it was to be a homeless person," Francis said during a speech at St. Patrick's Cath-

---

* Carol Kuruvilla, "Pope Francis Skips Lunch with Politicians to Be with Homeless in Washington, D.C."; *Huffington Post,* Sept. 24, 2015; http://www.huffingtonpost.com/entry/pope-francis-skips-lunch-with-politicians-to-visit-homeless-in-washington-dc_us_5603f27de4b08820d91bb9c1; accessed Oct. 14, 2016.

olic Church nearby—"what it was to start life without a roof over his head. I want to be very clear. We can't find any social or moral justification, no justification whatsoever for lack of housing. We know that Jesus wanted to show solidarity with every person. He wanted everyone to experience his companionship, his help and his love. He identified with all those who suffer, who weep, who suffer any kind of injustice. He tells us this clearly, 'I was hungry and you gave me food, I was thirsty and you gave me something to drink, I was a stranger and you welcomed me.'"

Named Person of the Year in 2013 by *Time* magazine, Pope Francis is widely considered to be one of the most charismatic leaders of our time. The pope's style is that of kindness charisma, as he is famous for his humility. Here are some of the ways Pope Francis conveys his charisma to inspire others, from *The Washington Post*.*

"WHO AM I TO JUDGE?"
Pope Francis's comments on homosexuality contrasted with those of his predecessors. In a wide-ranging talk, he reached out to gay people and said he wouldn't judge priests for their sexual orientation. "If someone is gay and he searches for the Lord and has good will, who am I to judge?"

---

* "Pope Francis's Acts of Humility," *The Washington Post;* https://www.washingtonpost.com/opinions/pope-francis-acts-of-humility/2013/07/25/4e7db41c-f49e-11e2-aa2e-4088616498b4_gallery.html?_ga=1.170267808.1274226675.1465870911#photo=4; accessed Oct. 14, 2016.

"I WILL WASH THE FEET OF OTHERS."
On Holy Thursday, reflecting a ritual based on Jesus's washing of the apostles' feet before his death, Pope Francis washed the feet of twelve criminal offenders. That included two women, one a Serbian Muslim. No pope had ever done this.

"I DON'T NEED A PALACE."
Instead of living in the opulent papal apartments, Francis opted to live in a Vatican residence alongside visiting clergy and lay people. "I'm visible to people and I lead a normal life—a public Mass in the morning, I eat in the refectory with everyone else, et cetera," he wrote to Father Enrique Martinez. "All this is good for me and prevents me from being isolated." A day after being chosen pope, he returned to his guest house, thanked the staff—and personally paid the bill.

"I'LL CARRY MY OWN BAG."
Francis caused a stir by carrying his own black hand luggage to his flight to Brazil on July 22, 2016. He even kept holding it while shaking hands with VIP well-wishers and while climbing the stairs to the jet's entrance.

"CALL ME FRANCIS."
The desire for humility extends to his name. Born Jorge Bergolgio, he took the papal name of Francis in honor of St. Francis of Assisi, who, after being raised in a wealthy family, gave up worldly goods and lived a life of poverty.

"WITH THE POOR, I WALK THE WALK."
Pope Francis made sure to visit slums such as those in Varginha during his trip to Brazil; the shantytown is so violent that locals call it Brazil's Gaza Strip. Weeks earlier, the pope invited 200 homeless people to dinner at the Vatican. Afterward, he gave each a gift pack with pastries, fresh fruit, and a rosary.

"WHY A BALCONY? I CAN SPEAK FROM MY DOORSTEP."
Unlike his predecessor, Pope Francis said he would spend most of the summer of 2016 at work in steamy Rome rather than at the papal summer residence in Castel Gandolfo. While at the mountainside retreat on July 14, however, he met crowds for prayer—right at the front door.

"I DON'T NEED A FANCY POPEMOBILE."
Whenever possible, Pope Francis has avoided the fortified Mercedes of his predecessor and opted for less expensive vehicles.

"REALLY, I CAN TAKE THE SUBWAY."
As a cardinal and archbishop of Buenos Aires, he lived in a small apartment rather than in the archbishop's palace, cooked his own meals, and used public transportation.

So let's look at how Pope Francis measures up on the five components of charisma.

1. Be Self-Confident
The pontiff demonstrates his self-confidence by daring to

be humble in the face of available opulence. It's not that he doesn't feel that he deserves to live in grandeur, it's just more in line with his values not to. It takes self-confidence to walk away from other people's expectations of you.

2. Tell Great Stories
Despite language barriers, the pope tells great stories. Reminding people that Jesus was homeless at his birth was a powerful way to connect the plight of homelessness with Christian heritage.

3. Use Body Language
Holding meetings at his front doorstep instead of from a high balcony indicates, literally, that he is on the same level as his followers and that his door is metaphorically open to them. In addition, he always seems to have a smile that goes all the way up to his eyes.

4. Make the Conversation about the Person You're Talking To
Whether he is kissing babies' heads or talking about a terrorist shooting, Pope Francis keeps the conversation on topic. Those who have been in his presence say that for the moments you're with him, you feel like the only person in the room.

5. Be a Good Listener
When transgender man Diego Neria Lejarraga met with Pope Francis in 2015, it was groundbreaking. The Catholic Church formally condemns sex change operations, and yet

when Diego wrote to the pope, the pontiff not only called him, but arranged for a visit.

Diego said, "In the presence of Pope Francis you feel loved, respected, embraced. I admired him before visiting, but that was nothing compared to the devotion I have for him now."*

How to Apply the C-Factor if You're a Charismatic Leader

Pope Francis exemplifies charismatic leadership in many ways. If you're in a leadership position, whether it's being the head of a large company or the leader of your local Girl Scout troop, here's how you can apply the C-Factor to increase charisma.

1. Be Self-Confident

Believe in yourself as a leader. Understand that leadership isn't always about being the person with the greatest technical skill. It's about being the person that others look to.

2. Tell Great Stories

Use the tools you learned in this book to tell great stories relating to your field. It's very easy to do an Internet search, look up the phrase "leadership anecdotes in _____"

---

* Tierney McAfee, "Touched by the Pope: Transgender Man Denounced by Parish Priest Says Visit with Pope Francis Gave Him a 'Safe Place' to Leave His Pain Behind," *People*, Sept. 17, 2015; http://www.people.com/article/pope-francis-transgender-man-meet; accessed Oct. 14, 2016.

and then fill in your area of leadership. The more you practice telling stories, the better you'll get at it.

3. Use Body Language
Practice having the body language of a leader. Whom do you respect as a leader in your field? Look at how they carry themselves and emulate their body language.

4. Make the Conversation about the Person You're Talking To
This is a critical skill for those in positions of formal authority. It's not about you telling your followers what you want. It's about talking with them—making your vision relate to the other person.

5. Be a Good Listener
Find ways to listen to your people. Call them on the phone and ask questions. Go to their offices. Encourage them to stop by yours. When you're listening to another, turn away from the computer and put the phone down. Make eye contact and let them know you really are hearing what they are saying. If someone communicates to you in writing, let them know you have listened by responding in a timely manner and acknowledging what they said.

8

The Charismatic Professional: Doctors, Lawyers, and Other Professionals

It was the middle of the Iraq war, and neurosurgeon and CNN reporter Sanjay Gupta was embedded with a group of Navy doctors. His role was to report on casualties of war, surgeries in the field, and other items of medical news in the middle of a horrific war-torn environment.

One day, his team came upon a boy who had suffered severe head wounds. The Navy surgeons turned to Sanjay and asked, "Will you help us?" Although the decision might seem difficult to some—after all, he was there to *report* on medicine, not practice it—it was a "no brainer" to Sanjay. "I'll do it." He was a neurosurgeon first and a reporter second.

When the news spread that he had performed surgery on the boy, criticism erupted alongside the gunfire. Sanjay writes:

When that story aired, I came under another sort of fire. "How can you be objective when you're standing shoulder to shoulder with Navy doctors?" Another newspaper wrote that I "crossed the line."

I disagreed. There's a different set of rules when it comes to saving lives. Nowhere does it say that when you put on your press credentials they are a bar to your humanity. My worlds of medicine and media have come crashing together quite a bit since then, most recently in Haiti. I operated aboard the USS Carl Vinson on a 12-year-old girl named Kimberly at the request of the U.S. military. Again, the criticism was leveled, and again I wasn't fazed by it, but rather happy that Kimberly, once near death, was alive and reunited with her father.*

These stories illustrate the challenges faced by the charismatic professional. In medicine, law, and other professions, charisma can look a little different than in, say, executive leadership. Leadership implies the sentiment "You are my leader and I follow you," whereas professionals are performing functional, consultative roles. "I am sick, so I am going to a doctor." "I need legal assistance, so I am going to a lawyer."

Remember our C-Factor equation: $C = f(P_1 * P_2 * E_x)$. Charisma is a function of Person One, Person Two, and The Environment.

---

* Sanjay Gupta, "Finding My Path in Life," *Guideposts;* https://www.guideposts.org/inspirational-stories/sanjay-guptas-inspirational-story?nopaging=1; accessed Oct. 14, 2016.

In order for a professional to have charisma, they need to have charismatic qualities, and to be able to influence the other person, within a certain environment.

How does Sanjay Gupta measure up in the areas of charisma?

1. Be Self-Confident

Self-confidence isn't just about feeling good about your ability to do something. It's also about knowing who you are at the core. Throughout his career in medicine and in broadcasting, Sanjay stayed true to his identity: "I am a doctor first." This enabled him to prioritize his actions to keep them in line with his values—even in the face of public criticism.

2. Tell Great Stories

Clearly, as a reporter, Sanjay has the ability to tell great stories—stories that connect people emotionally to the news he is reporting. For example, when giving talks, he tells a story about the time he met a young boy whose family had lost everything but still offered him some crackers to eat.*

"Here are people who truly had nothing at all but who offered me all that they had. How many times have I walked in this country where people have everything in the world and they won't give you the time of day," he

---

* "CNN Correspondent Dr. Sanjay Gupta Shares Experiences with UTPA Community," University of Texas–Pan American website, March 23, 2006; http://www.utpa.edu/news/2006/03/cnn-correspondent-dr-sanjay-gupta-shares-experiences-with-utpa-community.htm; accessed Oct. 14, 2016.

said, adding that he donates the money he receives from speaking engagements to an organization he founded in Sri Lanka that helps orphaned children there.

3. Use Body Language

Sanjay's body language conveys a combination of warmth and likeability along with trustworthiness and credibility. He has a large, warm smile that goes all the way up to his eyes. When he speaks, he uses his hands a lot, and shows viewers his palms, indicating openness. Voted one of *People* magazine's "Sexiest Men of 2003," he clearly has charismatic body language.

4. Make the Conversation about the Person You're Talking To

As a professional speaker, one of Sanjay's keys to success is to keep the topic of his talks focused on the audience. When talking to medical students, he relates to them by sharing stories of when he was in med school. When speaking to middle-aged mothers, he shares his own parenting stories. When talking to journalism students, he shares stories about that.

"He was charismatic yet humble," communications major Lynda Laurin commented on a 2006 presentation by Sanjay. "I could relate to him because I want to do a lot of things in my life; I hope I can prioritize like he does."

Hari Namboodiri, administrator of the McAllen Nursing and Rehabilitation Center, said he felt fortunate to be able to attend the presentation of such a world-renowned physician and journalist. "Dr. Gupta's speech was inspirational and thought provoking. I learned about three key elements of leadership—passion, profession, and performance. He is truly the personification of the American dream," he said.

5. Be a Good Listener

Typically, when we hear "Be a good listener," we envision this warm, empathetic face with big eyes looking at you while you're talking. While that is certainly one way of listening, Sanjay Gupta also illustrates a different kind. This is the kind of listening you do when someone tells you something meaningful, and you hear it and use it to pay the same message forward to others. Here's an example, where Sanjay is describing what a mentor told him as he was about to operate on a drunk driver who had caused the death of the child who had been in the car.*

"I felt like saying, 'Look, I'm not sure I'm cut out for this. Do I really want to be in a situation where I'm operating on this guy who ultimately killed his kid?' It took somebody who was more experienced and had been through it before to say, 'Look, take a day to get your head around it and realize that what you do is important. Everything is not going to turn out great, but don't measure yourself by the bad stories, measure yourself by the good ones.' It's not something I teach as a prescheduled lecture or discussion, but if something like that were to happen I have been blessed with good mentors and teachers myself, and I would convey some of those same lessons."

---

* Allison Kugel, "CNN's Sanjay Gupta: An Intimate Interview with the World's Doctor," PR.com, March 12, 2012; http://www.pr.com/article/1203; accessed Oct. 14, 2016.

It's clear from our discussion in this chapter that being a charismatic professional can have a deep, lasting effect. But not all of us are neurosurgeons or reporters for CNN. What does a charismatic professional look like in everyday life?

Bill and the DUI

Bill's teenage daughter has been arrested for driving under the influence of alcohol. Only seventeen at the time, Sadie wasn't supposed to be drinking at all, let alone driving intoxicated.

After getting Sadie out of jail on bond, Bill contacts an attorney. In reviewing the paperwork, it comes to their attention that the arresting officer forgot to sign and date the paperwork.

Bill tells his attorney, Michael, "I think we should go to court and fight this on a technicality. I don't want Sadie to lose her license because of one mistake, and we have a case here."

Michael can see that Bill is upset. "Bill, let's take a walk and talk about this." They go outside and start walking around the courtyard near the office. "Bill, I'm a dad," says Michael. "I understand wanting to protect our kids. But let me tell you a story. Once, about twenty years ago, there was a teenage boy who was in the same situation as Sadie. This boy drank too much at a party when he was only sixteen, tried to drive home, and ran his truck into a tree. He was arrested for DUI. This kid didn't have a dad, and his mom was too busy working three jobs to spend much time with him. So when the lawyer wanted to prove that the accident was caused by faulty brakes on the truck, the mom said yes. Long story short, this kid got off. Fast forward five years to college. The kid is at a party, drinks too much, and drives again. This time he isn't so lucky, and what he hit wasn't just a tree that wrecked his truck. It was a minivan with a mom and her two kids. One of the kids died, Bill. This mother had to lose one of her kids because this guy didn't learn his lesson the first time. You know who that guy was, Bill? It was me."

Michael stops and looks Bill in the eyes. "Can we try to get Sadie off on a technicality? Yes. Might we win? Yes. But is it the right thing to do? I don't think so."

In this anecdote, we can clearly see the C-Factor. This is a very charismatic speech on Michael's part. By going outside the office into a different environment, he is trying to control two of the variables in the C-Factor: himself—in the powerful story he told—and the environment. But whether or not Michael is successful in having charisma in this situation is also affected by Bill. If Bill isn't influenced by it, he is going to find another attorney to take Sadie's case.

How to Become a Charismatic Professional

Here are some suggestions on how to develop your own C-Factor as a doctor, lawyer, or some other professional, from an article by Dr. Kevin Campbell.* Although he

---

* Dr. Kevin Campbell, "Charisma In Medicine: Inspiring Others to Improve Patient Care," Nov. 18, 2013; https://drkevincampbellmd.wordpress.com/2013/11/18/charisma-in-medicine-inspiring-others-to-improve-patient-care/; accessed Oct. 14, 2016.

writes for physicians, the same lessons can be applied to anyone in the professional field.

1. Listen more than you talk—This one is tough for many physicians. In training we are taught to speak up when you know the answer. We are often motivated to provide quick results and to communicate them readily. We strive to quickly assimilate facts and produce a plan. However, much can be learned by listening—to patients, to families and to other health-care team members. When team members see that their ideas are considered by the leader, they tend to be more engaged and more productive. It doesn't matter who gets credit for the individual pieces of the puzzle. It's more important that the puzzle is completed successfully and the credit becomes a group effort.

2. Do not practice selective hearing—It is essential that physician leaders treat all team members with respect. Everyone has a role to play and it doesn't matter what title or status a particular individual may hold in the team hierarchy. By including everyone (and making each person feel like a contributor) we inspire hard work and more participation. Ultimately the patient receives much better care.

3. Put your stuff away—In the age of mobile phones, ipads and computers on the hospital wards distractions abound. However, when leading a team and listening to others express opinions and ideas, it is essential to leave the digital media in its holster—nothing makes others feel more unimportant than a disinterested leader. Take time to engage each person on the team and avoid the distractions of a text, a phone call, or a tweet.

4. Give before you receive—In medicine it goes without saying but be sure to put your patients and their families first. Within the care team, allow others to take credit and receive praise for a job well done before any is directed your way as the leader.

5. Don't act self important—Medicine breeds ENORMOUS egos—particularly in world-renown [*sic*] academic centers. To be more effective, we must put ego aside—forget the fact that you may have published half of the manuscripts in the medline search that the medical student just performed. Focus instead on others and what they bring to the team. Remember, we are all human—we are all connected.

6. Realize that other people are important—you already know what you know, you can't learn anything new from yourself. Listen to what others have to say—focus on their opinions and learn from their biases.

7. Shine the spotlight on others—Everyone feels validated by praise. There is never enough praise to go around. As the team leader make sure that you are adept at deflecting praise from yourself to those around you. Team members who feel that their work is recognized and appreciated as excellent tend to work harder and produce more.

8. Choose your words—How we go about asking others to perform tasks can greatly alter their perception of the task. If a task is presented as an obligation, it is viewed very differently than if it is presented as an opportunity or a privilege. By carefully choosing your words you inspire others and make them feel as though their position on the team is a critical component for success.

9. Do not discuss the failings of others—Let's face it, the hospital is a fishbowl and people gossip. However, nothing is more destructive to team dynamics that when a leader speaks negatively about a team member, a colleague or another physician. This behavior undermines morale and does not inspire confidence.

10. Admit your own failings—It is essential for teams and leaders to feel connected. Nothing promotes connection more than when a leader admits his or her own mistakes and failings to the group. However, when admitting a mistake it is essential that the leader set an important example—when admitting a failing also admit what was learned through the event and what corrective actions you plan to take to avoid the mistake in the future. This sets a wonderful example for self improvement for the team and at the same time promotes connectedness within the care team.

9

The Charismatic Entrepreneur

I was in my late twenties, so I had a business, but nobody knew who I was at the time. I was headed to the Virgin Islands and I had a very pretty girl waiting for me, so I was, umm, determined to get there on time.

At the airport, my final flight to the Virgin Islands was cancelled because of maintenance or something. It was the last flight out that night. I thought this was ridiculous, so I went and chartered a private airplane to take me to the Virgin Islands, which I did not have the money to do.

Then, I picked up a small blackboard, and as a joke, wrote "Virgin Airlines. $39." on it, and went over to the group of people who had been on the flight that was

> *cancelled. I sold tickets for the rest of the seats on the plane, used their money to pay for the chartered plane, and we all went to the Virgin Islands that night.*
> —Richard Branson

Richard Branson, the famed charismatic leader of the Virgin Group, is one of the richest people in the world. The Virgin Group's core businesses include retail operations, hotels, video games, book publishing, radio and television production, and of course an international airline. Branson is a perfect example of a charismatic entrepreneur (versus a charismatic leader), because his relentless drive for expansion causes him to take on one industry after another, starting businesses and then moving on.

Vanderbilt University professor Jane Robbins explores Branson's charisma in a 2009 blog posting.

> Richard Branson, CEO and founder of the megacorporation, Virgin Group, is very vocal about what he thinks works for his company. First, that good ideas come from everywhere, not just in the boardroom. Second, that his employees are central to his success, and finally that he has to use his authority as a leader.
>
> It is in his seemingly carefree spirit that he has no formal business headquarters, does not hold regular board meetings and supposedly doesn't know how to use a computer. This attitude does not mean that he isn't incredibly involved or busy. It is somewhat of an allusion [*sic*], but one that lends itself to a creative workplace.... By utilizing these in an open work environment Branson

has been able to foster a creative work environment that really does accept ideas from all levels. . . .

"Having a personality of caring about people is important," says Branson. "You can't be a good leader unless you generally like people. That is how you bring out the best in them." Because of his openness and empathy, it is apparent that he recognizes the importance of his employees. He goes on to say, "A company is people . . . employees want to know . . . am I being listened to or am I a cog in the wheel? People really need to feel wanted." Branson has built his brand by employing people he can involve in the process.

He is adventurous and curious, but also realizes he cannot agree to everything. Branson has noted how difficult it is to say no to his employees because he does not want to discourage their creativity. He explains that he had to learn how to say "no" and make tough decisions. . . . Branson had shaped his mission of fostering creativity.*

When you look at the qualities mentioned, you can see that a large part of Branson's success is due to his personal charisma. Remembering that charisma is a matter of being able to influence another person, it's clear that the respect that Branson has for the creative process and for his employees is a huge factor in his influence over them.

---

* Jane Robbins, "Richard Branson and the Virgin Group," Nov. 3, 2009; http://leadership theory3450.blogspot.com/2009/11/richard-branson-ceo-and-founder-of-mega.html; accessed Oct. 10, 2016.

In an interview with organizational dynamics writer Manfred Kets De Vries, Branson outlines some more of his philosophy. While he wasn't talking about charisma in particular, we can apply his comments to the C-Factor.

> My weaknesses really go back to the fact that I have spread myself too thin. In a purely business sense, I suspect that if I just wanted to maximize profits, I should have stayed more focused on one area and really concentrated on that one area. That's the conventional way, and I'm sure that's what most business schools teach. Perhaps it's right. But it wouldn't have been half as much fun.
>
> I must admit that I feel very much alive when I set out to achieve something. On reflection, it's really more the fight than the actual achieving. I love people and I just love new creative challenges. Some people ask, why keep battling on when you can take it easy? My reason, basically, is that I'm very fortunate to be in the position I am. I've learned a great deal and I've had great fun doing so. I'm in a unique position of being able to do almost anything I like and achieve almost anything I wish. I don't want to waste the position that I find myself in. I know that at age 80 or 90 I would kick myself if I just frittered away this second half of my life. I really do believe that fighting competition is exciting. . . .
>
> Basically, I admire anyone who takes on either the establishment or something like a mountain and succeeds or fails.

I sometimes wake up at night and lie there and think, "Is it all a dream?" Because it has been pretty good to date. It just seems almost too much for one man in one lifetime. So, if I am to reflect, I have been very fortunate to have so many wonderful experiences. Every day is fascinating. Every day, I am learning something new.*

Let's go back to the C-Factor equation: $C = f(P_1 * P_2 * E_x)$: charisma is a function of Person One, Person Two, and The Environment.

So in order for an entrepreneur to have charisma, they need to have charismatic qualities, to be able to influence the other person, within a certain environment. Let's take a look at Branson and apply the C-Factor.

First, he has the charismatic qualities needed. He's clearly self-confident, tells great stories (recall the opening story in this chapter), and is an excellent listener who focuses his conversations on the other person.

In addition, if you've ever seen Richard Branson, his body language exudes charisma. He dresses in very relaxed attire, has a very open body posture, and smiles a lot.

But you might be thinking, "Sure, I would be able to project an easy confidence like that if I were one of the richest people in the world."

---

* Manfred E.R. Kets de Vries, "Charisma in Action: The Transformational Abilities of Virgin's Richard Branson and ABB's Percy Barnevik," *Organizational Dynamics*, winter 1998, 7–11; http://citeseerx.ist.psu.edu/viewdoc/download?doi=10.1.1.467.3374&rep=rep1&type=pdf; accessed Oct. 10, 2016.

Let's take a look at the C-Factor as it applies to an entrepreneur with nothing more than a good idea.

Henry and the Hardware

Henry spent his career working for a telecommunications company. It was a huge company, and he was an individual contributor there, writing code for software programs. Henry made a good living, but wasn't satisfied working for a large corporation.

Like most people, the first thing Henry does in the morning is reach for his phone to check his messages. But he hates fumbling around for his glasses and trying to read the tiny print. His entrepreneurial mind always asks, "Is there a better way to do this?"

One night, Henry bolts awake with an idea for a product. What if there were a wall-mounted screen that, by remote control, mirrored a person's cellphone? Henry could sit in bed and scroll through his emails, Facebook, and other things on his phone, without having to wear glasses, get out of bed, or even touch his phone. And it would be priced in such a way that it would be far less expensive than a television or a computer monitor.

Energized, Henry spends his weekends making a prototype. His knowledge of software and hardware enable him to create a working example.

But having a great product isn't enough. Henry has to influence enough people to make, sell, and distribute his product. That's where his personal charisma comes in.

How to Apply the C-Factor if You're an Entrepreneur

1. Be Self-Confident

If you're an entrepreneur, you've got to have confidence both in your product, and in yourself. Your enthusiasm has to be contagious!

2. Tell Great Stories

This is a really essential skill for an entrepreneur. In Henry's case, he can use stories to engage potential partners and customers with his product. "Imagine it's Sunday morning, and you're not ready to get out of bed yet. Instead of reaching for your phone, all you have to do is reach for the remote . . . "

3. Use Body Language

Even if you don't yet have the wealth of Richard Branson or other successful entrepreneurs, you can still adopt their body language. Smile frequently, make good eye contact, and use open postures, and your perceived charisma will dramatically increase before you even open your mouth.

4. Make the Conversation About the Person You're Talking To

When you're an entrepreneur, it's important to connect with people one-on-one. Just as Richard Branson lets his people approach him with "crazy ideas," be open and approachable. Give people your full attention, and don't always be talking about your ideas.

5. Be a Good Listener

This is perhaps the most critical skill of an entrepreneur, because being a good listener allows you to identify opportunities. When Henry heard people saying, "I check my phone before I even get out of bed . . ." he was then able to have an idea of how to make the process easier.

10

The Charismatic Employee

It all started as an experiment.

In a *Fast Company* article, writer Art Kleiner describes how the Purina dog food plant in Topeka, Kansas wanted to create a new kind of organization—one without management.*

> Their idea: "unlearn" every traditional practice and design a plant from scratch to capitalize on (aspects) of human nature. Although decidedly skeptical, a General Foods vice-president uttered the fateful words: "Go ahead, you are free to fail."

---

* Art Kleiner, "Management Bites Dog Food Factory," *Fast Company,* June–July, 1996; http://www.fastcompany.com/26906/management-bites-dog-food-factory; accessed Oct. 11, 2016.

Sections of the plant painted in bright colors became natural centers where teams gravitated to compare notes—or to thrash out differences. There were no supervisors, only teams and team members who controlled plant operations. They hired new members, assigned shifts, set hours, and redesigned the placement of machinery. Everyone rotated through a wide variety of jobs. Significantly, they shared freely in information about the plant's finances and cash flow.

Without the overhead of middle managers, with an astonishingly low 2% absentee rate, and with a level of involvement bordering on ownership, the Topeka plant set performance records at General Foods. It became an example of the next-generation workplace: curious executives and business reporters lined up for tours in such volumes that they began charging admission.

Bill Goode, a vice president of human resources and quality for the company, says, "The system in Topeka has evolved to a much higher level than any of our other plants. We look at it as a model of where we'd like to go."

When most people think of charismatic leadership, they think of it as being top-down. In fact, when you search the term *charismatic employee*, the results only show articles and books that outline the impact of a charismatic leader on employees. Nothing comes up about the charisma of employees.

There's a concept in field of management called *emergent leadership*, where an individual within a group emerges as a leader because the formal leaders are either absent or insufficient in some way.

In an article in *The Leadership Quarterly*, author Anthony T. Pescosolido says that emergent group leaders are able to assume a leadership role by being the manager of group emotion.* In other words, a group faces some kind of problem or challenge and has a common emotion of ambiguity. No one is sure what's going on. But one person from within the group is able to manage the group's emotions, and they begin to look to that person as the informal group leader. Leader emergence and leader success are determined by several conditions, one of which is the emergent leader's degree of empathy.

Here's an example. A group of employees at an electronics store is just closing up, and management has gone home, when a robber bursts in and takes them all hostage. Locked in a storeroom in the back, the employees are all facing fear and uncertainty. "What are we going to do?" One employee, Cary, senses the group emotion, and says, "Guys, look. We are going to be fine. There are ten of us and one of him. Let's stay calm and figure a way out of this." By changing the emotion of the group, Cary has emerged as the leader in this situation.

Since we have defined the C-Factor so that charisma is a function of the qualities of one person—Cary—as seen by the other person(s)—the employees—in a particular environment—the hostage situation—Cary is clearly using his charisma, even though he is not a formal leader of the group.

---

* Pescosolido, Anthony T. "Emergent leaders as managers of group emotion." *The Leadership Quarterly* 13, no. 5 (2002): 583-599.

One doesn't have to be in a hostage situation in order to use charisma as an employee. Think about how much influence a person can have as an employee if they have the C-Factor. From getting a new coffee vending machine, to casual Fridays, or, in the case of the Purina factory, designing product packaging and having influence over budgetary issues, being a charismatic employee can effect meaningful change.

How can you use the C-Factor as an employee? Let's look at our five qualities.

1. Be Self-Confident
Clearly, in order to become an emergent leader, one needs to have a strong sense of self-confidence. Cary understands that the group was scared and doesn't know what to do. If he didn't have enough confidence to speak up, then he would never have emerged as the leader.

2. Tell Great Stories
One way a charismatic employee can emerge as the leader of the group is by being able to tell stories that convey his or her vision for something. You can envision the employees at the Purina plant telling stories about their dogs and experiences with packaging. The ability to tell great stories is a powerful way for charismatic employees to exercise influence.

3. Use Body Language
Imagine two employees at a team meeting. One is looking at his phone, leaning back in the chair, with a furrowed brow, or maybe even doodling on a note pad. The other

is leaning forward attentively, making eye contact with the other members of the group, and has an open, relaxed expression. Which employee would be considered more charismatic? Clearly, it's not only formal leaders who maintain charismatic body language. However, it is far more likely that a charismatic employee is going to be promoted to a formal leadership position.

4. Make the Conversation about the Person You're Talking To

As mentioned earlier, empathy is one of the core determinants of an emergent leader's success. Empathetic people are the ones who can sense the emotion of other people and stay focused on them.

5. Be a Good Listener

Part of being able to assess the emotion of a group is listening. In our robbery example, Cary listens to what the other employees were saying. In our Purina example, without the pressure of management, charismatic employees are able to listen to each other and share information freely.

How can you become a charismatic employee? Here are some suggestions.

- Get to know your coworkers. Talk to them. Ask about their weekends and their hobbies.
- Pay attention to your body language. Keep an open, engaged demeanor.
- Tell work-appropriate stories during breaks. If people enjoy listening to your stories, they'll like you more.

- Have an open door. Let your coworkers come to you with their problems and issues and listen empathetically.
- Find out what the group needs and then take steps to make it happen. Do people want to have food trucks in the parking lot once a month? See if you can make this happen.

11

The Charismatic Lover

She saw him the minute he walked into the room. Everyone in the place did, actually. There was something almost magical about him that made people flock to his side.

But she didn't rush to his side. Instead she stood back and watched him. She was afraid that the beating of her heart and the flush on her cheeks would give away her feelings. So she stood there.

As he made his way toward her, she felt rooted in place—as if her feet had grown into the ground. Then the crowd of people suddenly parted, and he looked at her. He had piercing blue eyes that seemed to instantly know everything about her. He held the gaze for a moment, and then the corners of his mouth turned up into a slight smile as he made his way toward her. The dance had begun.

There is a reason that romance novels are so popular. People want to read about dashing charismatic lovers. But you don't have to be Fabio to be a charismatic lover. In fact this chapter isn't about sex or lovemaking. It's about romantic partnerships.

The C-Factor can take you from being an average romantic partner to being a charismatic one. After all, the qualities that make a person charismatic are also the same qualities that make for a good romantic partnership.

According to a 2004 survey, marriages reaching the fifty-year mark made up only 6% of all marriages in the United States. Marriages that last seventy-five years or more are so rare that the U.S. Census Bureau doesn't even try to account for them.

Let's take a look at an extraordinary couple and apply the C-Factor to their relationship. It's the story of a California couple born on the same day and married for seventy-five years, who died only one day apart.* Helen and Les Brown died on July 16 and 17, 2013, respectively. Both were ninety-four.

According to the *Long Beach* (California) *Press-Telegram*, the couple also shared the same birthday of December 31, 1918, and met in high school. They eloped, marrying against their parents' wishes. Helen was from a working-class family, while Les was from a wealthier family, and neither family thought the love would last between them.

---

* Ashley Ruhl, "Long-Time Long Beach Couple Die a Day Apart," *Long Beach Press-Telegram*, July 25, 2013; http://www.presstelegram.com/general-news/20130725/long-time-long-beach-couple-die-a-day-apart; accessed Oct. 11, 2016.

Although they were born on the same day, the Browns were two very different people, according to their sons, who said their mother was very strict and their father was more laid-back. Like all married couples, they had some issues to work through during the years.

They were Jehovah's Witnesses, a faith that strengthened their marriage, the sons said. They reaffirmed their love for one another daily.

Zach Henderson, owner of the Ma N' Pa Grocery in Long Beach, said he saw the couple almost daily and called their relationship "a wonderful blessing."

"About a year ago, Helen had her hand on his face and they were cheek to cheek," Henderson said. "She said, 'Isn't he the most handsome man you've ever seen?' That's exactly how they were. They were full of love and passion."* Les, who had Parkinson's disease, and Helen, who had developed stomach cancer, were given a joint memorial service after seventy-five years of marriage.

Let's apply the C-Factor to this beautiful relationship to get some insight into why this marriage lasted as long as it did, and how you can apply it to your own romantic partnership.

1. Be Self-Confident

Given the fact that they eloped against their parents' wishes, Les and Helen had both self-confidence and confidence in the marriage. This isn't to say that every couple

---

* Gillian Monhey, via Good Morning America, July 27, 2013; http://abcnews.go.com/blogs/headlines/2013/07/couple-born-on-same-day-married-75-years-die-one-day-apart/, accessed Oct. 26, 2016.

that elopes or goes against the advice of friends and family has the C-Factor. But when you are in a romantic partnership, both partners have to have the confidence that the relationship is going to work out. In addition, each partner has to have the self-confidence to be their own person. With Les and Helen, they were different people, but they complemented each other.

2. Tell Great Stories

In a charismatic relationship, the couple tells positive stories about each other. In a bad relationship, they tell negative stories. "Isn't he just the handsomest man you have seen?" versus "If he leaves his socks on the floor one more time, I am going to scream."

To be a charismatic lover, tell great stories about each other and the relationship. Avoid the tendency to complain. Instead tell engaging stories that highlight and reinforce the positive qualities of the other person.

3. Use Body Language

One of the most common statements made by people who have been together for an extraordinarily long time is that they still express a lot of physical affection. Les and Helen are an example of that. "Helen had her hand on his face and they were cheek to cheek."

Holding hands, kissing, gazing into each other's eyes—even just regular touching—are ways to use body language to create a charismatic relationship.

4. Make the Conversation about the Person You're Talking To

We've all heard the stereotype of the woman who chooses the middle of an important football game to talk about "the relationship." Or the guy who is trying to tell his wife about his day at work, but she is distracted with the kids and dinner preparation.

In a charismatic relationship, each partner takes the time to focus on the other person. This isn't to say that 100% of the conversations are spent gazing into each other's eyes. But the charismatic relationship is one where each partner cares enough about the other person to make the conversation about that person on a regular basis.

5. Be a Good Listener

This is one of the most important keys to a good romantic relationship. It's not about being able to recite back what the other person is saying. It's about reading between the words and listening to the meaning.

For example, Mark comes home after a tough day at work. He's gotten his performance evaluation back, and it's not as good as it was last year. His wife, Stacy, stops what she's doing and sits down to listen to the words Mark is saying. But she also hears that he is scared of losing his job and not being able to support the family. Mark has never said that, but Stacy intuitively knows it. She lets Mark tell her what happened, walks over to him, and embraces him. She doesn't share her own concerns in this moment, but is fully present in what Mark is experiencing. Then she reassures him. "Honey, you are really good at your job. Are there some things you can change? Sure. But I know you and I know you can do this. We had a rough year last year with the move and Mom passing away. But next year is going to be better."

Again, there are several different types of charisma. Remember, *focus charisma* is characterized by presence. People with this kind of charisma give you the feeling that they are fully present and listening to what you say.

Visionary charisma is characterized by belief. People with this kind of charisma make others feel inspired or give others a sense of empowerment and belief in a better future.

Kindness charisma is characterized by warmth. People with this kind of charisma radiate total and complete acceptance of others.

Authority charisma is characterized by status and power.

In our story above, Stacy demonstrates several different types of charisma. She uses focus charisma when she stops what she's doing and sits down to listen to him. She demonstrates kindness charisma when she hugs him and accepts him and tells him that it's been a tough year. She then demonstrates visionary charisma by helping Mark to see a better future next year. You'll notice that authority charisma doesn't really apply here, as romantic partnerships usually occur among peers.

The romance novel example we gave at the beginning of this chapter is a good example of authority charisma.

"Charismatic people give the impression that they have a lot of power and also that they like you, or could like you, a lot," says author Olivia Fox Cabane.

In the next chapter, we'll take a look at what can happen when two charismatic lovers engage in the behaviors that lovers do. We'll look at charismatic families.

12

The Charismatic Family

In the long-running television show *Blue Bloods*, Tom Selleck plays Frank Reagan, the New York police commissioner and charismatic patriarch of a multigenerational family. He lost a son one year before the show's story line begins, and he lost his wife four years prior to that.

The Reagan children are all in the "family business" of law enforcement, with the sons as police officers and the daughter as an assistant district attorney. Henry Reagan, Frank's father, is a retired police commissioner. Every Sunday night, the entire clan gets together at the family home for dinner, where engaging debates about the law and morality take place. Devout Catholics, the family has shared vision, mission, and values.

The show is a powerful example of a charismatic family. Why is it important to look at—and build—charismatic families? The University of Missouri published research findings that show that many problems of individuals and society are related to dysfunctional family relationships.* For instance, early teen sexual acting out, youth suicide, teen pregnancy, runaways, substance abuse, childhood and adolescent depression, child abuse and neglect, family violence, and civil unrest are known to be aggravated by problems in the family.

By creating strong families that possess the qualities of the C-Factor, we can change the fabric of society. The qualities of charismatic individuals can be seen in groups too.

Writer Ron Hanson outlines nine qualities that are shared by successful families who are in business together.** As you're reading, you'll note that many of these qualities are the same as we see in individuals who have the C-Factor.

1. Team approach

Successful business families value family time together. Family events and celebrations are a priority. All members feel that they are stakeholders in the business and that their contributions are recognized and important to everyone.

---

* Saralee Jamison et al., "Family Strengths"; http://extension.missouri.edu/BSF/strengths/index.htm; accessed Oct. 11, 2016.

** Ron Hanson, "Nine Characteristics of a Strong Family Working Relationship," *Dairy Herd Management*, Aug. 2008; http://www.dairyherd.com/dairy-herd/tools-for-profit/9-characteristics-of-a-strong-family-working-relationship-113935429.html; accessed Oct. 11, 2016.

2. Effective communication
Family members communicate with each other. Furthermore, they take time to listen to each other and understand others' concerns. The feelings of others are important to them.

3. Family commitment
There is a sense of commitment to each other as a family, a strong bond of family loyalty. Everyone has a feeling of pride for their work and for what the family accomplishes together as a work force.

4. Family religious faith
Spiritual life is a part of family life. The common belief that they share gives the family the inner strength to get through difficult situations while holding the family together as a unit.

5. Crisis-coping skills
These families have learned how to deal with a crisis within the family and/or the business. Family members support and encourage each other during difficult times. The strength to overcome adversity comes from within the family itself.

6. Positive outlook
Strong families are positive families. They focus on the positive aspects of any situation and never become trapped by a negative outlook or attitude.

7. Mutual appreciation
Family members share their appreciation for each other. They are quick to share their personal feelings. These are caring families who recognize the efforts and contributions of others.

8. Family fun
There is a sense of humor in relationships among successful families. Personal kidding is taken in stride. Family members are quick to share a smile and want to get along with others. Family functions are fun times.

9. Strengthened ties and values
Strong families take the time to strengthen values and to reaffirm hopes and dreams as family members working together. These values are passed on from one generation to the next.

Here is a similar, though not identical list of what makes families strong. These traits have been found in families of different types, races, social backgrounds, nationalities, and religious beliefs. Again there are nine traits:

- Caring and appreciation
- Time spent together
- Mutual encouragement
- Commitment
- Communication
- The ability to cope with change
- Spirituality

- Community and family ties
- Clear family roles

Now let's take a look at the attributes of charisma and apply them to charismatic families.

1. Be Self-Confident
Charismatic families have family pride. Whether it's having a family slogan ("The Smiths never stay down for long!"), a family movie or song, or a common family hobby ("Nobody bowls better than we do!"), charismatic families exude self-confidence as a unit.

2. Tell Great Stories
"Remember the time that Billy got lost at Home Depot and Mom went on the loudspeaker to call for him?" "Tell us the story again of how you and grandpa met." "The coolest thing just happened to me at work!" Charismatic families have great family stories that they share and hand down from generation to generation. Even if everyone groans when Uncle Jimmy tells the same story every year at Thanksgiving, it's still a way for them to bond as a family unit.

3. Use Body Language
Charismatic families show their connection with body language as well. Religious families may hold hands as they say grace. They embrace each other and express affection in ways that are defined by the culture of the family. One family may fist-bump or have a family handshake; another

family may kiss each other on the cheek. In addition to expressions of affection, charismatic families also use body language to show solidarity. When a charismatic family walks into a room, others can tell that they are a family unit by how closely they walk together and how they touch and look at each other.

4. Make the Conversation about the Person You're Talking To

In some noncharismatic families, members of the family always tend to turn the conversation back to themselves. "That reminds me of the time when I made the winning touchdown." In charismatic families, family members focus on the other people in the family. Introverted family members are drawn out and everyone gets their turn to share.

5. Be a Good Listener

This might be the most important quality of the charismatic family. The family should be the place where one can safely express feelings and opinions and be able to feel heard. This is especially important with areas of conflict. In the *Blue Bloods* example, the family members are often on opposing sides of issues, but they still listen to the other side and treat each other with respect.

How can you build a charismatic family? Here are some suggestions.

- Spend time alone with each child at least once a week.
- Listen openly to each other, even if there is disagreement.

- Eat a meal together as a family at least once a week. Have family members carry out mealtime tasks.
- Be patient with your children. Respect their feelings and abilities.
- Encourage family members by asking them to talk about their successes.
- Hold family meetings where all family members can talk openly.
- Write a family mission statement. This should tell about your family's purposes and goals.
- Start family customs or traditions.

13

The Charismatic Change Agent

When I was 17, I read a quote that went something like: "If you live each day as if it was your last, someday you'll most certainly be right." It made an impression on me, and since then, for the past 33 years, I have looked in the mirror every morning and asked myself: "If today were the last day of my life, would I want to do what I am about to do today?" And whenever the answer has been "No" for too many days in a row, I know I need to change something.

Remembering that I'll be dead soon is the most important tool I've ever encountered to help me make the big choices in life. Because almost everything—all external expectations, all pride, all fear of embarrassment or failure—these things just fall away in the face of death, leaving only what is truly important. Remembering that you are going to die is the best way I know to avoid the trap of thinking you have something to lose. You are already naked. There is no reason not to follow your heart.

About a year ago I was diagnosed with cancer. I had a scan at 7:30 in the morning, and it clearly showed a tumor on my pancreas. I didn't even know what a pancreas was. The doctors told me this was almost certainly a type of cancer that is incurable, and that I should expect to live no longer than three to six months.

My doctor advised me to go home and get my affairs in order, which is doctor's code for prepare to die. It means to try and tell your kids everything you thought you'd have the next 10 years to tell them in just a few months. It means to make sure everything is buttoned up so that it will be as easy as possible for your family. It means to say your goodbyes.

I lived with that diagnosis all day. Later that evening I had a biopsy, where they stuck an endoscope down my throat, through my stomach and into my intestines, put a needle into my pancreas and got a few cells from the tumor. I was sedated, but my wife, who was there, told me that when they viewed the cells under a microscope the doctors started crying because it turned out to be a very rare form of pancreatic cancer that is curable with surgery. I had the surgery, and thankfully I'm fine now.

This was the closest I've been to facing death, and I hope it's the closest I get for a few more decades. Having lived through it, I can now say this to you with a bit more certainty than when death was a useful but purely intellectual concept: No one wants to die. Even people who want to go to heaven don't

The Charismatic Change Agent

want to die to get there. And yet death is the destination we all share. No one has ever escaped it. And that is as it should be, because Death is very likely the single best invention of Life. It is Life's change agent. It clears out the old to make way for the new.

Right now the new is you, but someday not too long from now, you will gradually become the old and be cleared away. Sorry to be so dramatic, but it is quite true.

Your time is limited, so don't waste it living someone else's life. Don't be trapped by dogma—which is living with the results of other people's thinking. Don't let the noise of others' opinions drown out your own inner voice. And most important, have the courage to follow your heart and intuition. They somehow already know what you truly want to become. Everything else is secondary.

—Steve Jobs, Stanford commencement address, June 12, 2005*

That speech was given more than ten years ago, and yet remains as inspirational as the day it was given. It's long been said that Steve Jobs' charisma was manufactured. Not false, mind you, but learned. If you look at his early talks, they're the way you would expect a computer guy to talk. But, as is evidenced by this talk, charisma clearly can be learned.

This type of charisma, which we will call *change agent charisma*, is the kind that people think of when they hear

---

* "'You've Got to Find What You Love,' Jobs Says," *Stanford News,* June 14, 2005; http://news.stanford.edu/2005/06/14/jobs-061505/; accessed Oct. 18, 2016.

the word *charismatic*. This is the person who can command a room and feel very relaxed at all times. When you're in their presence, you feel a sense of awe. This is the person who can get others—no matter their level or status—to listen to them. Sometimes it's in the voice, sometimes it's in the mannerisms, other times it's in their actions. It's the person who does the thing you think can't be done, but there they are—doing it.

How do they do this? By helping others to change their frames.

A frame is, in essence, a broad "macro" view of a given situation. It's as if your mind were unconsciously looking at things through a camera lens. It puts some things in and leaves other things out. A receiver can only hear or receive things that enter through the frame. And our frames are influenced by our gender, education, relationship with other person, assumptions, personal agenda, sense of efficacy, and more. The experiences we have in the world, the things we learn and observe, all lead to frames.

Very often our frames are unconscious, meaning that we aren't always aware of how our experiences are shaping our perceptions. A charismatic change agent helps you to shift your frame—to help you to see things differently, to raise your aspiration higher, to make you see that more things are possible than you ever believed.

How does personal development guru Tony Robbins get people to walk across hot coals in bare feet? By getting them to shift their frames about what they can do.

How did thought leader Warren Bennis become a

trusted adviser to seven U.S. presidents and change the entire field of leadership? By expressing his ideas in a way that gripped people at a deeper level and inspired them to think more deeply themselves.

Clearly, the charismatic change agent is able to affect others and inspire them to go out and change the world. No one can change the world himself, but the change agent can be the catalyst for others to do so.

How can you develop this kind of charisma? By combining two different kinds of leadership: *charismatic leadership* and *transformational leadership*.

Academia distinguishes between these two types of leadership. In a 2008 academic conference presentation, authors James Reagan McLaurin and Mohammed Bushanian Al Amri explained it this way.

> Charismatic leaders can be defined as those who have high self-confidence, a clear vision, engage in unconventional behavior, and act as a change agent, while remaining realistic about environmental constraints. Their key behaviors include role modeling, image building, articulation of goals, showing confidence and arousing follower's motives.
>
> Transformational leaders are those who stimulate interest among followers to view their work from new perspectives, generate awareness of the vision of the organization, develop followers to higher levels of ability and potential, and motivate colleagues and followers to look beyond their own interests toward those that will benefit the group. Their key behaviors include

empowerment, role modeling, creating a vision, acting as change agents, and making the norms and values clear to all.

Though there are similarities between the two concepts, there are also numerous differences. The main similarities are the focus on the vision, ideals, values and charisma from the leader's perspective. The major differences include charisma being one among the qualities of a transformational leader rather than the sole element, the effect of situational favorableness or uncertainty on both approaches, transformational behavior de-emphasizing charisma, the charismatic leader's possible self-centeredness and the probable negative effects of charismatic leadership.*

With the charismatic leader, the focus is on the person. The transformational leader focuses on the receiver and the environment. The charismatic change agent with the C-Factor encompasses the idea that charisma actually is a function of the person, the receiver, and the environment as a whole.

Let's take a look at Steve Jobs' commencement address within the context of our five qualities of the C-Factor.

1. Be Self-Confident

Steve Jobs' talk wasn't the self-centered kind of confidence that can signal the dark side of charisma. Instead, it was a

---

* James Reagan McLaurin and Mohammed Bushanian Al Amri, "Developing an Understanding of Charismatic and Transformational Leadership," *Proceedings of the Academy of Organizational Culture, Communications, and Conflict* 13, no. 2 (2008): 333–37.

humble confidence from a man who literally changed the world with his invention. To become a charismatic change agent, demonstrate confidence without arrogance and stay focused on sharing your vision with your followers.

2. Tell Great Stories
Clearly the commencement address excerpt provided examples of a good story. In fact the entire address included three such compelling stories. They moved the audience to change the frame about what is possible in their lives. By shifting the idea that death is the end to the idea that death is a catalyst for growth, the audience left with a greater impetus to change.

3. Use Body Language
Steve Jobs' physical appearance changed over time as well. His early photographs show him more as a computer nerd. By the end of his life, he wore his iconic black T-shirts and adopted the body language of a charismatic change agent. He went from a person who looked at his notes to one with an intense stare that captivated listeners.

4. Make the Conversation about the Person You're Talking To
In the commencement address, Steve was talking to college-aged adults. This is a different talk than he would have given his employees, and a different one than he would give to a group of peers. Yet the visionary tone and tenor of his talks were the same no matter whom he was speaking to.

5. Be a Good Listener
This is where being a transformational leader is essential. Typically, charismatic leadership is all about "this is how I see our future." Transformational leadership tends to ask more questions and listen more intently to the answers. In order to become an agent of change, one must clearly understand the status quo.

Conclusion: The Charismatic Life

Congratulations! You're almost finished with *The Power of Charisma*. You've learned what charisma is, how to cultivate it, and why it can help your life (and the lives of the people around you). You now know how to harness the power of charisma to inspire change. It's truly the greatest power you have.

When Traci and I created *The Top 2%*, we created an action plan so that people could implement the ideas they'd learned in the book. It's pretty clear that knowledge doesn't lead to change; different *behavior* leads to change. Or, as they say, "If nothing changes, nothing changes."

As you move forward after reading the book, continue to practice using the C-Factor. In fact, we have a Thirty-Day

C-Factor Challenge, which will give you the opportunity to practice applying the C-Factor to your life.

Remember in the beginning of the book you took the C-Factor Quiz? We said you would have an opportunity to take it again. Now is that time! Also, remember that we said that since a person can be charismatic and not know it, it's a good idea to have trusted friends and family take the quiz for you. You'll find a blank copy of the quiz on the next page.

Are you ready to "C" what you've learned? Turn the page!

The C-Factor Quiz Revisited

For each of the questions, rate yourself on a scale from 1 to 10, with 10 meaning "This totally describes me," and with 1 meaning "This doesn't describe me at all."

1. When I set a goal, I can clearly imagine what it will be like when I've achieved it.

    1 2 3 4 5 6 7 8 9 10

2. I speak with conviction and passion.

    1 2 3 4 5 6 7 8 9 10

3. I'm comfortable asking other people to do things for me.

    1 2 3 4 5 6 7 8 9 10

4. When I walk into a room, I get an immediate sense of the mood of the room.

    1 2 3 4 5 6 7 8 9 10

5. When I'm on the phone with someone, it's evident right away how I am feeling.

    1 2 3 4 5 6 7 8 9 10

6. I wouldn't ask someone to take a risk that I'm not willing to take myself.

    1 2 3 4 5 6 7 8 9 10

7. When I meet someone, I make eye contact and smile genuinely.

    1 2 3 4 5 6 7 8 9 10

8. People tell me their problems and ask for my advice.

    1 2 3 4 5 6 7 8 9 10

9. I've been told that I am overconfident at times.

    1 2 3 4 5 6 7 8 9 10

10. I tell great stories.

    1 2 3 4 5 6 7 8 9 10

11. When someone is talking to me, they feel as if they are the only person in the room.

    1 2 3 4 5 6 7 8 9 10

12. People feel comfortable to be themselves around me.

    1 2 3 4 5 6 7 8 9 10

13. I enter a room with confident body language.

    1 2 3 4 5 6 7 8 9 10

14. I'm not afraid to make fun of and laugh at myself.

    1 2 3 4 5 6 7 8 9 10

15. I am comfortable with who I am.

    1 2 3 4 5 6 7 8 9 10

Scoring

To find your score, add together the numbers you chose for each question.

1. _____
2. _____
3. _____
4. _____
5. _____
6. _____
7. _____
8. _____
9. _____
10. _____
11. _____
12. _____
13. _____
14. _____
15. _____

Total: _____

Results

15–45: A BIT SHY

If you scored in this range, you probably tend to be socially introverted and a bit shy. But never fear: charisma is a learned skill. By the end of this book, you are sure to have moved up the scale a bit.

46–90: IT DEPENDS

You're shy at times, but when you want to, you are capable of opening up and interacting with others. It all depends on the situation. The tools and techniques you'll learn in this book will help you feel more confident in your charisma.

91–134: MOSTLY CONFIDENT

Most of the time, you feel a deep sense of confidence. You like yourself, and others do too. Sometimes you wish you could be more persuasive. Once you learn the C-Factor, you'll be able to be naturally charismatic.

135–150: MAGNETIC CHARM

You are one of those rare individuals who possess natural charisma. You light up a room when you walk in, and people tend to gravitate to you. You tell great stories and can laugh at yourself. But you check your ego at the door. True charisma isn't about what others think of you, but how you make them feel.

The C-Factor Challenge: A Thirty-Day Program to Gain Charisma in Every Area of Life

Congratulations! You've finished *The C-Factor* and now have a better understanding of how to become more charismatic. Now it's time to put your knowledge to use with the C-Factor Challenge! In the next thirty days, you'll apply skills in the five key areas of charisma: "Be Self-Confident"; "Tell Great Stories"; "Use Body Language"; "Make the Conversation about the Person You're Talking To"; and "Be a Good Listener." (Since they are related, we're combining the last two areas into one.)

Before we get started, let's do a visualization exercise. What would being more charismatic mean for you? How would it feel to walk into a room and have that magnetic "It Factor" that charismatic people have? Just take a moment and close your eyes and visualize a situation where you're being charismatic. That is what you'll be like in just thirty days.

Week One: Be Self-Confident

Day 1: Set Your C-Factor Goal

On this first day of the C-Factor Challenge, you'll look ahead and identify somewhere that you can demonstrate your mastery of the C-Factor. Maybe it's a networking event or a sales call or a job interview. You could sign up to give a talk or some other situation where you'll have an opportunity to demonstrate a greater level of charisma than you have in the past.

Once you've picked your goal, write it in your calendar, and then write it here:

Day 2: Physical Exercise

In this first week of the challenge, we are going to increase your level of self-confidence. You might be surprised that physical exercise is the activity for the second day.

Research shows that people who exercise have a greater sense of confidence than those who don't.* In one study, people with the highest levels of physical activity, cardiovascular fitness, and muscular strength experienced less stress than those who had lower levels. They also scored higher on tests of "mental resources"— how energetic, capable, and confident they felt about their daily tasks.

So for the next twenty-eight days, engage in some form of physical activity. You don't have to train for a marathon to experience the benefits of exercise. Just spend twenty to thirty minutes every day doing something physical. Go for a walk or a bike ride. Do some yoga. Lift some weights or engage in resistance training. Or just jump rope with your kids or play fetch with your dog. Don't overthink it, just get out there and move! (Check with your physician if you have any physical constraints.)

---

* Oili Kettunen, *Effects of Physical Activity and Fitness on the Psychological Wellbeing of Young Men and Working Adults: Associations with Stress, Mental Resources, Overweight, and Workability.* Ph.D. dissertation, University of Turku, Finland, 2015; http://www.doria.fi/handle/10024/103576?trk=profile_certification_title; accessed Oct. 11, 2016.

Day 3: Make a List Of Your Positive Traits

What a better way to build your confidence than to create a list of your positive traits? Oftentimes we tend to exaggerate the negative parts of our personalities and minimize our strengths. Here is a list of several positive personality traits. Which ones fit you? Think of a specific example of a time when you have demonstrated that quality. Doing so helps ground the perception with reality. It's one thing to tell yourself, "I am a compassionate person." But it's even more meaningful when you say, "I demonstrated compassion when I gave that homeless man my umbrella."

After you're done, ask a trusted friend or loved one what *they* think your positive traits are, and to give you examples of each.

- adaptable
- adventurous
- affable
- affectionate
- agreeable
- ambitious
- amiable
- amicable
- amusing
- brave
- bright
- broad-minded
- calm
- careful
- charming
- communicative
- compassionate
- conscientious
- considerate
- convivial
- courageous
- courteous
- creative
- decisive
- determined
- diligent
- diplomatic
- discreet
- dynamic
- easygoing
- emotional
- energetic
- enthusiastic
- exuberant
- fair-minded
- faithful
- fearless
- forceful
- frank
- friendly
- funny
- generous

gentle	nice	romantic
good	optimistic	self-confident
gregarious	passionate	self-disciplined
hard-working	patient	sensible
helpful	persistent	sensitive
honest	pioneering	shy
humorous	philosophical	sincere
imaginative	placid	sociable
impartial	plucky	straightforward
independent	polite	sympathetic
intellectual	powerful	thoughtful
intelligent	practical	tidy
intuitive	proactive	tough
inventive	quick-witted	unassuming
kind	quiet	understanding
loving	rational	versatile
loyal	reliable	warmhearted
modest	reserved	willing
neat	resourceful	witty

Make sure you do this exercise today, because you'll need it tomorrow.

Day 4: Clarify Your Values

You might wonder what clarifying your values has to do with the C-Factor. After all, isn't that some lofty personal development exercise? While values clarification is generally part of personal growth, it can also help build confidence. When you know very clearly what you stand for, and what you do not, you are better able to align your behavior with your values. When your behavior is in alignment with your values, it builds self-confidence. It also enables you to become a role model for other people. Since charisma is about having influence over others, it is important to be able to clearly convey your values. Then you can influence others who share those values to live by them.

For example, in our exercise yesterday, you went through the positive personality qualities. If you consider yourself a person who values compassion, and have identified times when you were compassionate, you can share stories of those times. "It was one of the coldest days of the year. Bitter rain was coming down, and I saw this man, in a wheelchair, at a bus stop, holding a soggy newspaper over his head in a futile attempt to deflect some of the rain. I sat at the red light, in my warm car, with a full belly, and knew I had to do something . . . "

Personal development expert Brian Tracy describes how he clarified his values.

Write Out Your Key Values

When I first began this values clarification exercise some years ago, I wrote out a list of 163 qualities that I aspired to. I think I eventually came up with every virtue, value or positive descriptive adjective that referred to personality and character in the dictionary. And I agreed with all of them. I felt that they were all important and I wanted to incorporate every single one of them into my character.

Focus on Very Few Core Beliefs

But then reality sets in. I realized that it is very hard to learn even one new quality, or to change even one thing about myself, let alone dozens of things. So I scaled down my ambitions and began narrowing the values down to a small number that I could manage and work with. Once I had settled on about five core beliefs, I was then able to get to work on myself and start making some progress in character development.

Select Your Five Key Values

You should do the same. You should write down the five values that you feel are the most important for you to live by. Once you have those five values, you then organize them in order of priority. Which is the most important value in your hierarchy of values? Which would be second? Which would be third, and so on?*

From the list you generated yesterday, select your five core values and organize them in terms of priority. What is most important to you? It is in these values that the source of your charisma lies.

Day 5: Do a Good Deed

One of the best ways to feel good about yourself is to do something good for someone else. Here is a list of forty

---

* Brian Tracy, "Clarify Your Values"; http://www.briantracy.com/blog/sales-success/clarify-your-values/; accessed Oct. 11, 2016.

"random acts of kindness." Pick one and do it today. (If you're feeling generous, do more than one!)

1. Donate money to charity.
2. Send a thank you note to someone who has made a difference in your life.
3. Take treats to the Humane Society.
4. Give someone a free car wash.
5. Tape popcorn to Redbox for movie night.
6. Take cookies to the fire station.
7. Take flowers to a nursing home.
8. Take someone's dog for a walk.
9. Leave quarters at the laundromat.
10. Buy coffee for a police officer.
11. Take cupcakes to nurses at the hospital.
12. Take crayons and coloring books to the waiting room at the hospital.
13. Take balloons to sick patients in the hospital.
14. Buy a drink at a vending machine and leave it for the next person.
15. Donate old cellphones to women's shelters.
16. Put money in the donation box at McDonald's.
17. Pay for someone in line behind you at Starbucks.
18. Push up grocery carts.
19. Give someone a gift card.
20. Give a food donation for a feed the hungry program.
21. Pick up neighbors' trash cans.
22. Give a juice box donation to preschoolers.
23. Read to preschoolers.
24. Give a clothes donation to charity.

25. Make dinner for a sick friend.
26. Give blood.
27. Thank the mail carrier.
28. Thank the trash person.
29. Donate recycling.
30. Sends care package to soldiers.
31. Buy a one-hour massage for a single mom.
32. Donate blankets for the homeless.
33. Take lunch to a friend who is at work.
34. Clean the house for an elderly person.
35. Pay for two kid's admission to a museum.
36. Make a care bag with toiletries for homeless people.
37. Leave a gift card in a favorite children's book.
38. Hand out peanut butter sandwiches to homeless people.
39. Donate books to the library.
40. Buy a gas card and give to someone at the gas station.

Day 6: Reframe Your Negative Qualities

Everyone has negative qualities. It's part of being human. But, as we mentioned, often we tend to focus on our negative qualities and minimize our positive ones.

What if, instead of doing that, we were able to reframe our negative qualities? In other words, think of a time when you made a mistake, did something stupid, or demonstrated a quality that you don't have to have. Then reframe it. Think back on why you did what you did. Are you really just a jealous spouse, or was there a legitimate reason for your feelings?

Today think of five of the qualities that you don't like about yourself. Then reverse the statement by adding in or taking out the word *not* and then asking yourself "under what conditions would the second sentence be true?" For example, "I am late all the time" would become "I am NOT late all the time." Then ask, "Under what conditions am I NOT late all the time?" Pretty soon you realize, "I'm not late ALL the time. I'm on time when taking the kids to school and when I have a doctor's appointment."

Another example might be "I'm not a very good sister." That becomes "I'm a very good sister." "Under what conditions am I a very good sister?" "Well, there was that one time when she got sick and I cleaned her house. That was a good sister thing to do."

Now it's your turn. First, write the sentence that reflects your bad quality. Then take out or add the word *not* to make the sentence have the opposite meaning. Then ask yourself, "Under what conditions would that be true?"

Day 7: Dress Your Best

By now you've been exercising for several days. You're already probably starting to feel better and more confident about your appearance.

Today we are going to take it to another level. Dress your best! This doesn't mean you dress in a tuxedo to go to Taco Bell. But it does mean that you stop wearing pajamas to the mall (if you do that). Take a few minutes every morning and choose clothes that will make you feel confident. If you don't think you have anything nice to wear, do yesterday's exercise and challenge that assumption. Or take a few dollars and go to the thrift store and buy some clothes that fit and make you feel good about yourself. It's amazing what dressing nicely can do for your confidence level.

Day 8: Clean Up Your Environment

Today's activity isn't about saving the earth, although that's a nice thing to do. Instead, it's about boosting your confidence by cleaning your home and workplace. It doesn't have to take five hours, either. Home cleaning expert Marla "Flylady" Cilly suggests doing a one-hour "power clean" to straighten up your home.* She suggests setting a timer and spending no more than ten minutes on each of the following tasks:

Vacuum
Dust
Quick mop
Polish mirrors and doors
Purge magazines and catalogs
Change sheets
Empty all trash cans

These are not "deep cleans" but quick fixes. Do this today, and see how much better you feel about yourself!

---

* Marla "Flylady" Cilly, "What Is Weekly Home Blessing Hour"; http://www.flylady.net/d/br/2012/05/14/what-is-weekly-home-blessing-hour/; accessed Oct. 17, 2016.

Week Two: Tell Great Stories

This week we are going to focus on the second skill that charismatic people have—the ability to tell a great story. Don't worry that you'll need to become a professional speaker. Just focus on being able to deliver an anecdote or story in an engaging way.

Day 9: Keep a Story Journal

Stories are everywhere. From blogs to Facebook posts, things overheard at your local diner to a commercial on television, we come in contact with stories every day. But more often than not, we don't remember them.

"I was in a car wash . . . where was it again? And there were these people . . . I seem to recall they were surfers. Or, no. Skaters. Right. And they were joking about putting their skateboards through a car wash." That's not the most effective way to tell a story.

Here is the story again, but told with a clear recollection of the details.

"Last summer, I was waiting for my car to go through the car wash when four older teenagers sat next to me. These were typical California kids, with their skateboards and those hats with the short brims. I'm looking in the window watching my car go under the soap sprayer, and their car is behind mine. It was a funny sight, my Lexus right in front of a very old Volkswagen. One of the guys says to me jokingly, 'Excuse me, ma'am. Do you think they would mind if I took my skateboard through the car wash?'"

Now that's not the most earth-shattering story, but if you'd written down the details, you'd be able to better remember the small things that make it interesting.

For this week (and maybe beyond) carry a notepad with you and jot down things you hear that would make a great story. If you are in a library and overhear two elderly women talking about how they met their husbands, and you find the story interesting, jot it down.

Doing this accomplishes two things. First, it helps you to become more detail-oriented and trains your brain to better remember the little things. Second, you'll build a library of stories to draw from when you're communicating.

Day 10: Use Good Story Structure

The skateboard example from yesterday is also a good illustration of another element in good storytelling. Make sure that your story has a good structure. Here are some elements of good story structure.*

1. Clear moral or purpose. There's a reason why you're telling this story to this audience at this time. In our skate-

---

* Kristi Hedges, "How to Tell a Good Story," *Forbes*, Dec. 11, 2013; http://www.forbes.com/sites/work-in-progress/2013/12/11/how-to-tell-a-good-story/#cb9afe15dae9; accessed Oct. 11, 2016.

board story, this isn't clear, as we don't have the context. But when you're telling a story, make sure that the listener doesn't wonder, "Why is he telling me this?"

2. Personal connection. The story involves either you or someone you feel connected to. In our skater story, the narrator is telling a story that happened to her.

3. Common reference points. The audience understands the context and situation. In our story, most people have been to a car wash and have watched their cars go through the soap sprayer. And most of us have met teenage skateboarders.

4. Detailed characters and imagery. Have enough visual description that we can see what you're seeing. In our story, we can envision the clothes the skaters are wearing. The narrator points out the contrast between the two cars. And then there is an implied image of the young man going through a car wash on his skateboard.

5. Conflict, vulnerability, or achievement we can *relate* to. Similar to point number four: show us the challenges. This wasn't an element of that in this particular story, because it was so brief. But had the story gone on longer, the narrator would have connected the story to her larger point.

6. Pacing. There's a clear beginning, ending, and segue back to the topic. Our story began with the cars going through the car wash and ended with the image of a skateboard doing the same thing.

Tomorrow we'll talk a little more about the elements of a good story. But for today, start to be aware of the stories you hear and tell, and see which elements are present and which are missing.

Day 11: The Order of the Story

Again, using our silly skateboard example, how effective would it have been if the punchline were told in the beginning? It wouldn't have been! The order of the story is a critical part of storytelling. We have all been at a party somewhere when someone is telling this long-winded story that has too much background. Don't be that guy.

Here are some suggestions for structuring the order of your stories, from the Art of Charm website.

> First, remember that every story starts *before* the main event. Why were you in the situation that you were in to begin with? What key information does the audience need to appreciate the rest of the story? *That's* where the story begins. You need to tee up the story that you're going to tell before you start telling it. This shouldn't be your life story, but you should succinctly explain how you got into the situation you're about to discuss.

Once you've done that, you need to think about the logical order in which you tell the story. That's often—but not always—the important events of the story in the order they happened. But sometimes it makes sense to back up a bit and fill the listener in on some piece of background information that wouldn't have made sense at the beginning of the story. And while some small details that aren't totally relevant to the story can be thrown in for emotional effect, you don't want to get bogged down in irrelevant information.

Once you've got your skeleton, start thinking about what fills it in. Who else is involved in your story? What does the listener need to know to understand the other characters in your story? Fleshing out the other people in your story is one simple way to make the overall story more compelling and relatable. Even if the person listening can't relate to you, they might be able to enter the story through another character.

While every story is different, most stories follow a general pattern. You start with the background, then tell the listener how the story started. This is the event that triggers the story to begin. The action should rise throughout until it reaches a dramatic peak—a point of no return—also known as the climax. You then drive from the climax to the final events of the story. After that, you can briefly discuss the consequences of the story. This is called the denouement, and it's the bookend of the narrative.

Following this general pattern is crucial to being a good storyteller. Otherwise, you'll find that most people, who have an intuitive sense of what makes a good story, will grow restless.*

Today, then, take one of the story ideas from your story journal and write it out, using what you've learned so far this week.

Day 12: Choose Your Level of Disclosure

Have you ever been talking to someone and they gave you "TMI" or "too much information"? Doing so can really make the listener uncomfortable. But you need to have *some* level of self-disclosure, or the audience won't relate to the story. Here are some thoughts on the level of self-disclosure, also from the Art of Charm.

> Basically, the higher the level of self-disclosure in the story, the deeper the connection you're going to make with your listeners. But there's also the risk that you might expose too much and embarrass yourself. Alternately, you might come across too strong and alienate or even offend your listeners. Becoming a good storyteller is about mastering that trade-off over time.
>
> Ultimately, that's a calculated risk you're going to have to make when you tell a personal story. But I've broken it down into three basic levels to help you get a feel for what you're getting yourself into:

---

* "Making Friends through Storytelling"; Art of Charm website; http://theartofcharm.com/self-mastery/how-to-tell-a-great-story/?hvid=4mBaIC; accessed Oct. 11, 2016.

- **Light disclosure** involves amusing anecdotes about yourself and the world around you. Light disclosure tends to be brief, with a clearly defined beginning, middle, and end. This tends to be a quick little anecdote about something funny or interesting that happened to you in the course of your daily life.

- **Medium disclosure** gets more serious, because it involves your beliefs, opinions, and ideas about the world. This is a riskier proposition, because there's someone out there who's bound to be affected by your thoughts and feelings. Medium disclosure is best for the time after you have established some degree of rapport with your listeners. You need to feel reasonably confident that, even if they don't agree, they won't be looking for the nearest exit.

- **Heavy disclosure** is, as you might guess, the riskiest and most difficult kind of storytelling. This is where you begin sharing your fears, insecurities, failures, and pain points with your listeners. There's a twofold risk with heavy disclosure. First, you might come across as needy or validation-seeking. Second, your listeners might laugh *at* you rather than *with* you. You want to save heavy disclosure for situations where you feel very safe sharing deeply personal and painful parts of your life. You also want your storytelling ability to match the level of disclosure, which is a matter of practice.

For the most part, when you're out at a bar, business networking event, or other place where you're meeting new people, you'll want to stick mostly to light self-disclosure with maybe a little bit of medium self-disclosure once you've started to make a connection. Heavy self-disclosure is either for people you already know very well or people that you want to become trusted confidants and companions.*

Today take a look at your story journal and determine the appropriate level of disclosure for each of the ideas you've noted. Is there a way to tell the story to increase or decrease the level of disclosure?

Day 13: List Some Stories about Yourself

So far this week, you've been focusing on developing ideas for *new* stories. But you weren't just born this week. You have a lifetime of stories waiting to be told. Today spend some time thinking of stories you could tell in the following areas:

CHILDHOOD AND TEENAGE YEARS
- Your family
- Pets
- Vacations and camp
- School and teachers
- Hobbies
- Friends and enemies
- Learning to do something

---

* "How to Tell a Great Story," The Art of Charm; http://theartofcharm.com/self-mastery/how-to-tell-a-great-story/?hvid=3q1eB7; accessed Oct. 18, 2016.

ADULTHOOD
- Falling in love
- Getting married
- Jobs and job interviews
- Moving to a different residence
- Travel
- Interesting people you've met
- College, university, and graduate school
- Having children

Day 14: Voice Work

In the '90s hit television show *Friends*, one of the characters, Janice, has a whiny, nasal voice that is the source of irritation for her boyfriend, Chandler. In fact, her iconic voice is one of the things that most people remember about the series.

While having an annoying voice and laugh makes for a funny television bit, if you're trying to become a more effective speaker, you don't want to be remembered for your funny voice. You want to be remembered for your story!

To that end, here are five tips for improving your voice, adapted from an article in *Fast Company*.

1. Slow Down

One of the most important things you can do to improve the clarity of your message is to slow down, says Katie Schwartz, president of Durham, North Carolina speech coaching firm Business Speech Improvement. People tend to speak quickly when they're nervous or unsure of what they're saying. Speaking more slowly not only improves your audience's comprehension of what you're saying, but it also makes you sound more confident and more in control.

A good benchmark is to speak slowly enough that, if you were reciting a phone number, the person listening to you would be able to write it down. Practice your speech speed by reciting a long string of numbers, and writing them in the air as you do so. That's just about the perfect cadence.

2. Breathe

If you breathe shallowly in your chest instead of deeply into your abdomen, your voice will sound weaker and possibly jittery. It can be tough to remember to breathe deeply when you're nervous or stressed, but taking full, relaxed breaths will improve the depth of your voice and can help you sound more confident, says Kate DeVore, founder of Total Voice, a Chicago-based speech coaching firm.

3. Watch Your Posture

The way you sit or stand could affect your speech. Standing or sitting straight allows you to breathe properly and gives your voice greater strength and clarity, says DeVore.

Moving your head a bit can also make a difference. If you lift up your chin and tilt your head slightly, you can cut some of the resonance and make your voice sound more clear. If your shoulders are tight and hunched up toward your head, "you're cutting out big chunks of your voice's potential potency," she says.

4. Hydrate

Keeping yourself well-hydrated also helps the quality of your voice, DeVore says. If you're drinking coffee, soda, or wine throughout the day instead of water, your vocal cords might not have the moisture they need to make your voice sound the best it can be.

"The vocal cords need to be fairly pliable because of how fast they vibrate," DeVore says. "For women they vibrate an average of 200 times per second, and for men it's about 120 times per second."

5. Watch Your Pitch

Voices with high pitch or a nasal quality often reflect nervousness or insecurity on the speaker's part, Schwartz says. Using the right vocal pitch helps you be a more effective communicator. You can find your perfect pitch by saying, "uh-huh" as if you were casually saying "yes" to a friend's question. Schwartz says the pitch of your voice when you speak should match the "uh."

6. Avoid Yelling

Love cheering on your team at the top of your lungs? That's not exactly great for your vocal cords, Schwartz says. Yelling can strain them and make it difficult for you to speak. In the worst cases, yelling can lead to vocal nodules, or bumps on your vocal chords.

Now it's your turn. Practice saying the following sentences with the inflection on different words, as well as speaking slowly, confidently, and with the right volume.

I was born in Australia. (You, on the other hand, were born somewhere else.)

I **was** born in Australia. (How dare you imply that I wasn't?)

I was **born** in Australia. (I'm a native, not a newcomer.)

I was born **in** Australia. (Not outside Australia.)

I was born in **Australia.** (Not in New Zealand.)*

Day 15: Practice Telling Stories

Today is the day your storytelling skills come together. Find an opportunity today to tell a story. Prepare first by doing this:

1. Pick a story from one of the exercises this week.
2. Write it out, including only the elements you wish to include.
3. Practice it alone, in your car, or in front of a mirror. Repeat this as many times as needed until you're comfortable.
4. Tell the story to someone else!

---

* Gwen Moran, "Six Simple Ways to Improve the Way You Speak," *Fast Company*, Sept. 16, 2014; http://www.fastcompany.com/3035634/how-to-be-a-success-at-everything/6-simple-ways-to-improve-the-way-you-speak; accessed Oct. 11, 2016.

Week Three: Use Body Language

Imagine that twin brothers walk into a crowded room. The first brother enters the room looking down at the ground, shoulders slightly hunched forward, with short, shuffling steps. Someone says to him, "Hey, Dan," and he looks up, does the head nod that indicates he's heard them, and then, rubbing his forehead and sighing, keeps walking.

His brother, on the other hand, enters the room with confidence. Walking tall, with a confident stride, head up, looking around the room, he smiles at people. When someone says, "Hey, Dave," he makes eye contact, shakes their hand, and says, "Hi, there! Good to see you again."

Which of these two men will be perceived as having more charisma? Clearly, Dave. Even though they are twins, with identical physical features and clothing, one man exudes charisma and the other doesn't. What's the difference? Body language.

This week we are going to work on having charismatic body language. These tips come from former FBI agent and body language expert Joe Navarro in his book *What Every Body Knows*.

Day 16: Mirror Practice

Mirroring is a behavior where one person consciously or subconsciously imitates the gestures, speech pattern, or attitude of another. Have you ever found yourself doing this instinctively? When we're speaking to an older person, for example, we tend to slow down our speech, raise the volume, and enunciate clearly. "HELLO, MRS. BROWN. HOW ARE YOU TODAY?" And when we're interacting with a baby, we tend to mirror their facial expressions. They stick out their tongues, and we do too.

Today, practice mirroring the body language of some people, and see if they feel more psychologically comfortable with you. With others, use the *opposite* style and see what happens.

So for example, at the office, if you're talking to someone at the coffee machine, adopt the same body language as they have. Hold the cup in the same hand as they do. Stand with your legs as they have them. Make the same level of eye contact and facial expressions. You don't have to be weird about it; just subtly mirror their body language.

Then, with someone else, do the opposite. If you're in an elevator, face the people instead of the door. Or cross your legs and notice how strong the urge is to uncross them.

Just play around with mirroring and see what happens.

Day 17: Head Tilt

The way we hold our heads can be a way of expressing emotion. Think about it. When we lean forward with our heads, we are showing interest. Leaning back indicates reservation or disbelief or shock. And when we tilt our heads to one side or the other, it conveys empathy and understanding.

So today, when someone comes to you with a problem, try giving a little head tilt as the person talks to you. It makes the individual feel much more appreciated. It makes you appear to be much more open, and it makes for a very much more comfortable environment.

Day 18: Take a Stand

Another way to exude charisma is the way that we stand. If you want to convey power and authority, stand with your legs slightly apart and your hands in the steeple position (with your hands and fingers pointing upward and touching each other) in front of you. How does this feel?

Now contrast this with another, less confident position. Stand with your feet together and your thumbs inside your pocket. Feels different, doesn't it?

Then, look around at people whom you consider charismatic. Think of celebrities, athletes, businesspeople, or people in your personal life. How do they convey charisma with the way they stand? Practice mirroring that today.

Day 19: Avoid Looking Nervous

As we saw in the example with Dan and Dave, body language can convey that we are nervous. Joe Navarro calls certain types of behavior "pacifiers" because they are used to soothe ourselves when we feel uncomfortable.

A charismatic person avoids these kinds of behavior.

Today, see if you catch yourself, or others, engaging in the following:
- Rubbing the forehead
- Pulling on the hair
- Rubbing the nose
- Massaging the nose
- Pulling on the upper lip
- Stroking the chin
- Massaging the ears
- Pulling on the earlobes
- Twirling a pencil
- Mangling a paperclip
- Playing with a rubber band
- Rubbing the fingers
- Playing with jewelry or clothing (twisting a ring or pulling on a necklace)

Day 20: Smile

We've established that a person can tell within just a few seconds whether or not another person is being genuine. One of the key ways we do this is through the smile. A genuine smile goes up through the eyes and lights up the whole face. A "social smile" is one that only involves the lips and teeth.

Today we are going to see this in action. First, give someone a social smile, and see how he or she reacts.

Then, later, give someone a genuine smile. If you're not feeling particularly smiley, think of something that makes you happy, and then smile. See the difference?

For the rest of the day, smile at people, even if you don't feel like it. Smiling conveys that you are happy, confident, and approachable.

Day 21: Observe

Become an observer of nonverbal behavior wherever you go. What behaviors are you seeing at home, school, work, church, and other venues? In particular, begin to notice behaviors that are associated with comfort and those that are associated with discomfort.

Here are some categories of nonverbal behavior to watch.

Body movements (kinesics), for example, hand gestures or nodding or shaking the head.

Posture, or how you stand or sit, whether your arms are crossed, and so on.

Eye contact, where the amount of eye contact often determines the level of trust and trustworthiness, but is also heavily culturally dependent.

Closeness or personal space, which determines the level of intimacy. Again, this is heavily culturally dependent.

Facial expressions, including smiling, frowning, and licking the lips.

Physiological changes, for example, sweating or blinking more when nervous.

Day 22: Be Visible

Today be more visible as a means of communicating that you care. Use the things you have practiced this week to create a sense of connection between you and the people around you. Mirror their body language and vocal expressions. Smile. Make eye contact, and mirror their level of personal space. Keep practicing these things, and you'll be more like Dave than Dan.

Week Four: Make the Conversation about the Person You're Talking To and Be a Good Listener

In this, the last week of the C-Factor Challenge, we will finish our work with the charismatic qualities by combining two skills: the ability to make the conversation about the person you are talking to, and to become a good listener.

Day 23: Identify Your Listening Role Models

Oprah Winfrey. Larry King. Football player Peyton Manning. Jimmy Carter. These are some of the names that come to mind when you think of good listeners. But good listeners are everywhere. The woman who cuts your hair. The neighbor who helps walk your dog. Your twelve-year-old daughter. Who are the people in your life that you consider good listeners? Write their names down, and identify what makes them good listeners.

Name	**What They Do**

Day 24: Practice Response Generators

Part of being a good listener is asking questions that generate a response that is better than "yes" or "no." For example, "Did you like the movie?" could elicit a one-word response. But "tell me about the movie" is likely to generate a longer answer and give you a better chance to listen.

Today, with the people in your personal life, use the following expressions and see if they elicit a different response than you usually get.

- Oh?
- In what way?
- How so?
- Tell me more . . .
- Give me an example. . .

Day 25: Nonverbal Listening

The next few days are going to have you engaging in some fun exercises to help you become a better listener.

Today is all about nonverbal listening. Listen to all sounds around you: a refrigerator humming, a keyboard clicking, an air conditioning system rumbling. Listen to the distant (and not so distant) traffic noise; any airplanes flying by? Listen to people working, people hammering, people mowing the lawn. Listen to people talking, laughing, or crying. Listen to your own noises, your own breathing. What is the "vibe" around you?

Day 26: Sympathetic Disagreement

One important key in becoming a good listener is resisting the response to become defensive in a disagreement. To counter this, practice what is called *sympathetic disagreement*.

This exercise can be used with a partner or spouse. One person makes a statement. Then the second person repeats the part of the statement that they agree with, and then politely object to one specific part of it.

For example:

Larry: "I love chocolate donuts."
Michelle: "I love chocolate donuts, but they are really fattening."

The purpose of this exercise is to practice listening during disagreement.

Day 27: Check Your Assumptions

Very often when we listen to others, we have hidden biases or make assumptions without knowing it. How often have you had it happen where you hear something and automatically assume that it means one thing, and then you get some information that totally shifts your frame?

Biologically we are hardwired to prefer people who look like us, sound like us, and share our interests. *Social categorization* is the process whereby we routinely and rapidly sort people into groups. This preference bypasses our normal, rational, and logical thinking. We use these processes very effectively (we call it intuition), but the categories we use to sort people are not logical, modern, or perhaps even legal. Simply put, our neurology takes us to the very brink of bias and poor decisionmaking.

So if bias is hardwired, does this mean there's nothing we can do? Not at all. It's just a matter of becoming more aware of the possibility that your bias can influence what you're hearing.

Here are some tips for checking your assumptions and hidden biases when you are listening to others.

- Develop and nurture "constructive uncertainty." In other words, tell the other person, "Feel free to disagree with me" to establish a norm whereby it's OK to disagree.
- Develop the capacity to use a "flashlight" on yourself to help identify a bias; this in turn will help you appropriately act on it.
- Understand and redirect beliefs; don't try to suppress them.
- Explore awkwardness or discomfort by asking yourself, "What is triggering me in any particular situation?"*

---

* Adapted from resources developed by Howard Ross for presentation at NYS SHRM Diversity and Inclusion Conference, Oct. 2013.

Day 28: Be Fully Present (Let There Be Silence)

One of the greatest things you can do when listening is to just be present for another person, without the need to fill in the silences.*

Today, when listening, remain present with the person to the very end of the conversation, rather than starting to pick up your phone or look through papers on your desk as the person is leaving. Give them their full moment with you.

Furthermore, when you listen attentively, without distraction, you are more likely to notice gaps. You can probe the gaps gently, pause, and help people share what was left unsaid. Listen also for how people express themselves. Not everyone is comfortable talking about things as they are. Some people's style is to skirt around issues rather than be outspoken. Help them out. "It's been somewhat challenging" might mean "I am angry because goals for this project keep changing." When you listen for the subtext, you can do your part by drawing attention to the elephant in the room. You end up having an entirely different conversation.

---

* Bruna Martinezzi, "The Third Ear: A Powerful Tool to Becoming a Better Listener," American Express Open Forum, Aug. 12, 2013; https://www.americanexpress.com/us/small-business/openforum/articles/the-third-ear-a-powerful-tool-to-becoming-a-better-listener/; accessed Oct. 12, 2016.

Day 29: Practice Humility

The most powerful expression of charisma is the ability to listen with humility. Putting one's own ego aside and being open to learning from the other person can be an incredibly powerful means of influence.

Today, practice humble listening.

- Let down your defenses. Stop thinking of how you're going to react and simply entertain the possibility that the other person might be right.
- Recognize the value of the other person's words.
- Acknowledge your mistakes.
- Take responsibility.
- Verify that you understood the other individual.
- Inspire good listening skills in others.

Day 30: Use the C-Factor

$$C = f(P_1 * P_2 * E_x)$$

Charisma is a function of the qualities of Person One times the qualities of Person Two, affected by The Environment.

Today is the day it all comes together! You've read the book. You've taken the quizzes. You've done twenty-nine days of exercises and applications. Go back to the C-Factor goal you identified on Day 1 of the challenge. You now have everything you need to accomplish that goal. Now go out in the world and be charismatic!

The most dangerous leadership myth is that leaders are born—that there is a genetic factor to leadership. This myth asserts that people simply either have certain charismatic qualities or not. That's nonsense; in fact, the opposite is true. Leaders are made rather than born.
—Warren Bennis

Index

A

Academy of Management Journal, 9
Ace Ventura: Pet Detective (movie), 6
achievement, in story structure, 148
"Adrift at Sea" exercise, 31–37
Al Amri, Mohammed Bushanian, 123–124, 124*n*
Ali, Muhammad, 5
analogies, 57, 59–60
anecdotes, 57, 60, 152–153
animation, of voice, 42–43
Antonakis, John, 9*n*, *42n*
appearance, 144–145
Apple Computer, 119–121
appreciation, in family charisma, 114

arms, 45–46
　arms akimbo, 45
　crossing, 46
　regal position, 46
Art of Charm website, 149–153
Aschburner, Steve, 40
assumptions, checking, 166–167
athletes, professional, 39–42, 43–44
authentic charisma, 21
authority charisma, 10
　body language, 11, 21, 42–51
　communicating authority, 59, 60
　of decisive/satisficer unifocus decision makers, 29, 31, 36
　faking, 11, 20–21

authority charismam *(con't.)*
  lover charisma, 108–109
  status in, 37
autocratic leadership, 18–19

B

Baker, S., 20*n*
Balthazard, Pierre A., 37*n*
belief, in visionary charisma, 37
Bell, R. Mark, 61*n*
Bennis, Warren, 122–123, 170
biases, checking, 166–167
Bieber, Justin, 68
Blue Bloods (TV program), 111, 116
body language, 39–51, 70, 158–163
  arms, 45–46
  in authority charisma, 11, 21, 42–51
  in C-Factor Challenge, 158–163
  categories of, 162
  in change agent charisma, 125
  comfort displays, 45, 46, 47, 49, 50
  in employee charisma, 100–101
  in entrepreneur charisma, 93, 95
  facial expression. *see* facial expressions
  in family charisma, 115–116
  gestures, 43–44
  head tilt, 159–160
  in leader charisma, 75, 77, 82, 93, 95
  legs, 44, 45, 160
  in listening, 165
  in lover charisma, 106
  mirror practice, 158–159
  observing, 162
  pacifiers, 160–161
  posture, 155, 162
  sitting, 45
  stance, 160
  visibility, 163
  voice, 42–43, 154–157
  walking, 44
body movements (kinetics), 162
Branson, Richard, 89–93, 95
breathing, in voice work, 155
Brousseau, Kenneth, 26–37
Brown, Helen and Les, 104–108
Bryman, Alan E., 62
Bush, George W., 62
Business Speech Improvement, 154–155

C

C-Factor (charisma)
  assumptions about, 7–11
  benefits of, xvi–xvii
  components of, 70

dark side of. *see* dark side of charisma
environment and, 69–70, 145
exercises. *see* C-Size exercises
importance of, xv–xvi
as learnable skill, 9–10, 56–61
mind in. *see* charismatic mind
nature of, 4–6, 56, 67, 91
self-perception of, 6–7. *see also* C-Factor Quiz
styles of. *see* charismatic styles

C-Factor Challenge, 127–128, 135–170
body language, 158–163
C-Factor goal, 136
conversation about the other person, 164–170
listening, 164–170
self-confidence, 137–145
storytelling, 146–157

C-Factor equation, 67–70, 80, 93, 169–170

C-Factor Quiz, xix–xxiii, 129–133

C-Size exercises
"Adrift at Sea," 31–37
communication charisma, 59–61
focus, 11–12
handshaking, 48–49
social media reciprocity, 22

Cabane, Olivia Fox, 10, 42, 109
Campbell, Kevin, 85–88
Carrey, Jim, 6
Carter, Jimmy, 164
Casella, E D., 5n
change
emotions of group, 99
observing physiological, 162
preventing, 20–21
change agent charisma, 119–126
C-Factor, 124–126
charismatic leadership, 123–124
frame shifts, 122–123
Steve Jobs, 119–121, 124–126
transformational leadership, 123–124
characters, in story structure, 148
charisma. *see* C-Factor (charisma)
Charisma Myth, The (Cabane), 10
charismatic leadership. *see also* leader charisma
nature of, 123
transformational leadership *versus*, 124

charismatic leadership tactics
    (CLTs), 9–10, 56–61
  compare and contrast, 58,
      60
  connect, 57, 59–60
  engage and distill, 58–59,
      60
  reflect sentiments of
      group, 59, 60
  set high goals, 59, 60
  show integrity, 59, 60
charismatic mind, 23–38
  charisma styles. *see*
      charismatic styles
  Driver Decision Style
      Model, 26–37
  nature of, 23–25
  neuroscience, 37–38
charismatic styles, 8–10
  authority charisma. *see*
      authority charisma
  focus charisma, 10, 36,
      46–49, 108
  introversion, 8, 10, 116
  kindness charisma, 10–11,
      37, 108
  visionary charisma, 10,
      29, 31, 37, 108
Chicago Bulls, 39–42,
    43–44
Cilly, Marla "Flylady," 145,
    145*n*
Clinton, Bill, 5
Clooney, George, 5

closeness, 162
clothing, 144–145
coherent neural circuits, 37–38
Collins, Colleen, 3–4
comfort displays, 45, 46, 47,
    49, 50
commitment, in family
    charisma, 113
communication charisma,
    53–63
  C-Size exercise, 59–61
  in charismatic leadership,
      75–77, 82–87
  charismatic leadership
      tactics (CLTs), 9–10,
      56–61
  in crisis management,
      61–63
  family, 113
Community Action Team
    (CAT), 13–14
community leaders, 71–77
compare and contrast,
    communicating, 58, 60
complaints, 106
Conant, Lloyd, 24
conflict, in story structure,
    148
Conger, J. A., 62
connection, communicating,
    57, 59–60
consensus building exercise,
    31–37
contrasts, 58

conversation about the other person, 70
  in C-Factor Challenge, 164–170
  in change agent charisma, 125
  in employee charisma, 101
  in entrepreneur charisma, 93, 95
  in family charisma, 116
  in leader charisma, 75, 77, 82–83, 95
  in lover charisma, 107
corporate leaders, 71–77
crisis management, 61–63
  employee charisma, 99, 100, 101
  family charisma, 113

D

Daily Show, The (TV program), xiii
Dalai Lama, 10
dark side of charisma, 17–21
  faking authority charisma, 11, 20–21
  narcissism, 17–19
  preventing change, 20–21
  unethical charisma, 18–20
decision styles. *see* Driver Decision Style Model

decisive/satisficer uni-focus decision makers, 29, 31, 36
DeVore, Katie, 155–156
Diana, Princess, 8
Diaz, Cameron, 7–8, 30, 69
disagreement, sympathetic, 166
disclosure level, 151–153
dress, 144–145
Driver Decision Style Model, 26–37
  "Adrift at Sea" exercise, 31–37
  decisive/satisficer uni-focus, 29, 31, 36
  flexible/satisficer multi-focus, 29, 36
  focus, 27–29, 31, 36
  hierarchic/maximizer uni-focus, 28–29, 36
  information use, 26–27, 28–29, 31, 36
  integrative/maximizer multi-focus, 29, 31, 36
  operating style, 29–31
  role style, 29–31
Driver, Michael J., 26–37

E

ego involvement, 87
emergent leadership, 98–102
emotional contagion, 43–44
empathy, 101, 102

employee charisma, 97–102
    C Factor, 100–102
    crisis management, 99, 100, 101
    emergent leadership, 98–102
    Purina plant, 97–98, 100
engage and distill, 58–59, 60
entrepreneur charisma, 89–96
    Richard Branson, 89–93, 95
    C-Factor, 95–96
    Henry, 94
environment
    charisma and, 69–70
    cleaning up, 145
ethical charisma
    as authentic, 21
    nature of, 17–18
    unethical charisma *versus,* 19–20
Ewing, Patrick, 40
exercise, physical, 137
eye contact, 95
    in employee charisma, 100–101
    in handshaking, 48
    observing, 162
eyebrows/eyebrow flash, 49, 50
eyes, 49
    smiling, 50, 95

F

Facebook, 22, 54
facial expressions, 43
    eyebrows, 49, 50
    eyes, 49, 50, 95
    observing, 162
    smiling, 49, 50–51, 95, 114, 161–162
family charisma. *see also* lover charisma
    Blue Bloods (TV program), 111, 116
    C-Factor, 112–116
    tips for building, 116–117
Fast Company, 97–98, 154–157
Fenley, Marika, 9*n,* 42*n*
FlexBrain Method, x–xi
flexible/satisficer multi-focus decision makers, 29, 36
focus, 27–29
    C-Size exercise, 11–12
    multi-focus decision makers, 27–29, 36
    uni-focus decision makers, 27–29, 31, 36
focus charisma, 10
    hands in, 46–49
    lover charisma, 108
    presence in, 36
frames
    changing, 122–123, 143–144
    nature of, 122

Francis, Pope, 71–76
Freeman, Morgan, xv
Friedman, H., 5n
Friends (TV program), 154

G

Gates, Bill, 10
General Foods Purina factory, 97–98, 100
gestures, 43–44, 45–47. *see also* body language
   arms, 45–46
   hands, 46–49
goals
   C-Factor, 136
   communicating, 59, 60
good deeds, 141–143
Goode, Bill, 98
gossip, 88
Gupta, Sanjay, 79–84

H

hands, 46–49
   focus charisma, 46–49
   jazz hands, 47
   steepling, 47
handshaking, 47–49
   C-Size exercise, 48–49
   eye contact, 48
   politician's handshake, 48
Hanson, Ron, 112–115, 112n
Hare Krishna, 17
Harvard Business Review (HBR), 9–10, 56–61

Hatfield, Elaine, 43n
head tilt, 159–160
hearing, selective, 86
heavy disclosure level, 152
Henderson, Zach, 105
hierarchic/maximizer unifocus decision makers, 28–29, 36
Hitler, Adolf, 5
Hodges, Kristi, 147n
hostage situation, 99, 100, 101
Hughes, Howard, 8
humility, 88, 92, 169
humor
   in family charisma, 114
   self-deprecating, 60–61
Hunsaker, Phillip L., 26n
hydration, 156

I

imagery, in story structure, 148
influence charisma, 39–42
information use, 26–27, 28–29
   maximizers, 26–27, 28–29, 31, 36
   satisficers, 26–27, 28–29, 31, 36
Ingham, Harrington, 68–69
Instagram, 22
integrative/maximizer multifocus decision makers, 29, 31, 36

integrity
- communicating, 59, 60
- ethical charisma, 17–21

introversion, 8, 10, 116

J

Jamison, Saralee, 112n
jazz hands, 47
Jesus, 6, 71, 73, 75
Jobs, Steve, 119–121, 124–126
Johari Window, 68–69
Johnson, Magic, 5
Jones, Jim, 5
Jordan, Michael, 39–42, 43–44

K

Kelley, R. E., 19n
Kennedy, John, 5
Kets De Vries, Manfred E. R., 92–93, 93n
Kettunen, Oili, 137n
kindness charisma, 10–11
- lover charisma, 108
- warmth in, 37

kinetics (body movements), 162
King, Gayle, xiii
King, Larry, 164
Kleiner, Art, 97–98
Kugel, Allison, 83n
Kunz, Phillip, 15–17
Kuruvilla, Carol, 71n

L

Laurin, Lynda, 82
Le, Yen-Chi L., 43n
leader charisma. *see also* authority charisma
- Bill, 84–85
- body language, 75, 77, 82, 93, 95
- Richard Branson, 89–93, 95
- charismatic *versus* transformational leadership, 123–124
- community leaders, 71–77
- conversation about the other person, 75, 77, 82–83, 93
- corporate leaders, 71–77
- emergent leadership, 98–102
- entrepreneurs, 89–96
- Pope Francis, 71–76
- Sanjay Gupta, 79–84
- listening, 75–76, 77, 83–84, 86–87, 93
- professional leaders, 79–84
- religious leaders, 8, 10, 71–77
- self-confidence, 74–75, 76, 81, 93, 95
- storytelling, 75, 76–77, 81–82, 84–85
- tips for, 85–88

visionary charisma, 10, 29, 31, 37
Leadership Quarterly, The, 99–102
Leeds, Ed, 7–8
legs
  crossing, 45
  sitting, 45
  stance, 160
  walking, 45
Liechti, Sue, $9n$, $42n$
light disclosure level, 152–153
Lightner, Candy, xiv
LinkedIn, 54
listening, 70
  assumption check, 166–167
  avoiding digital media, 86–87
  bias check, 166–167
  body language, 165
  in C-Factor Challenge, 164–170
  in change agent charisma, 126
  in employee charisma, 101–102
  in entrepreneur charisma, 93, 96
  in family charisma, 116
  giving before you receive, 87
  importance of, 86–87
  in leader charisma, 75–76, 77, 83–84, 86–87, 93
  in lover charisma, 107–108
  nonverbal, 165
  response generators, 165
  role model identification, 164
  selective hearing *versus,* 86
  sympathetic disagreement, 166
Long Beach (California) *Press-Telegram,* 104–108
Lopez, S. J., $5n$
lover charisma, 103–109. *see also* family charisma
  Helen and Les Brown, 104–108
  C-Factor, 105–106
  romance novels and, 103, 108
Luft, Joseph, 68–69, $68n$

M

MADD (Mothers Against Drunk Driving), xiv
Manning, Peyton, 5, 164
marriage. *see* family charisma; lover charisma
Martinez, Father Enrique, 73
Martinezzi, Bruna, $168n$
maximizers, 26–27
  multi-focus style, 29, 31, 36

maximizers *(con't.)*
    uni-focus style, 28–29, 36
McAfee, Tierney, 76*n*
McConaughey, Matthew, 5
McConnell, John, xv
McLaurin, James Reagan, 123–124, 124*n*
medium disclosure level, 152
metaphors, 57, 59–60
mirror practice, 158–159
mistakes, admitting, 88, 92, 169
Monhey, Gillian, 105*n*
Monroe, Marilyn, 4
moral, in story structure, 147–148
Moran, Gwen, 157*n*
Moses, 6
Mothers Against Drunk Driving (MADD), xiv
multi-focus decision makers, 27–29
    maximizers, 29, 31, 36
    satisficers, 29, 36
Musk, Elon, 10

N

Nahavandi. Afsaneh, 21, 21*n*
Namath, Joe, 5
Namboodiri, Hari, 82–83
narcissism, 17–19
Navarro, Joe, 44–51, 158–163
Neria Lejarraga, Diego, 75–76
neuroscience, coherent neural circuits, 37–38
Newman, Paul, 4
Nightingale-Conant, 24
Nightingale, Earl, 23–25
nonverbal communication. *see* body language; facial expressions
norm of reciprocity, 15–17, 22

O

Obama, Barack, 5, 11
observing body language, 162
operating style, 29–31
Osteen, Joel, 10

P

pacifiers, avoiding, 160–161
pacing
    story structure, 148–149
    voice work, 154–155
Paxson, John, 40
personal space, 162
personality traits, positive, 138–139
Pescosolido, Anthony T., 99–102
Peterson, Suzanne J., 37*n*
Pinterest, 22
Pippen, Scottie, 41
pitch, in voice work, 154, 156
politician's handshake, 48

Porter, Lyman (Port), 8, 10
positive outlook
   employee charisma, 99, 100, 101
   family charisma, 113
   lover charisma, 105
   positive personality traits, 138–139
   reframing negative qualities, 143–144
posture, 155, 162
power of charisma, 14–15
praise, 87
presence
   in focus charisma, 36
   in listening, 168
Presley, Elvis, 3–4
professional charisma, 79–88
   Bill, 84–85
   C-Factor, 81–84
   Sanjay Gupta, 79–84
   tips, 85–88
public speaking. *see* storytelling; voice work
purpose, in story structure, 147–148

Q
questions, rhetorical, 58

R
Rapson, Richard L., 43*n*
reciprocity, norm of, 15–17, 22
reflecting sentiments of group, 59, 60
regal position, 46
relationships. *see* family charisma; lover charisma
religious faith, in family charisma, 113
religious leaders, 8, 10, 71–77
   C-Factor, 74–76
   Pope Francis, 71–76
response generators, 165
Restauri, Denise, 70*n*
rhetorical questions, 58, 60
Rice, Condoleezza, 5
Riggio, R. E., 5*n*
Robbins, Jane, 90–91, 91*n*
Robbins, Tony, 10, 122
Roberts, Julia, 5
role style, 29–31
romance novels, 103, 108
Ross, Howard, 167*n*
Rudd, Justin, 13–14
Ruhl, Ashley, 104*n*
Russell, Joyce E. A., 17–19, 19*n*

S
sales and selling, charisma in, 14–15
satisficers, 26–27, 29
   multi-focus decision makers, 29, 36
   uni-focus decision makers, 29, 31, 36

Schwartz, Katie, 154–155, 156
selective hearing, 86
self-confidence, 70
   in C-Factor Challenge, 137–145
   in change agent charisma, 124–125
   clean environment, 145
   dress, 144–145
   in employee charisma, 100
   in entrepreneur charisma, 93, 95
   in family charisma, 115
   good deeds, 141–143
   in leader charisma, 74–75, 76, 81, 93, 95
   in lover charisma, 105–106
   physical exercise, 137
   positive personality traits, 138–139
   reframing negative qualities, 143–144
   values, 139–141
self-deprecating humor, 60–61
self-importance, 87
self-perception, 6–7. *see also* C-Factor Quiz
Selleck, Tom, 111
Siegfried and Roy, 8
silence, 168
similes, 57, 59–60
sitting, 45
smiling, 49, 50–51, 161–162
   eyebrows and, 49, 50
   eyes and, 50, 95
   fake, 50
   in family charisma, 114
social categorization, 166–167
social media, reciprocity exercise, 22
spiritual life, in family charisma, 113
sports, 39–42, 43–44
stance, 160
status, in authority charisma, 37
steepling hands, 47
Stewart, Jon, xiii–xiv
Stewart, Tracey, xiii–xiv
story journals, 146–147
story structure, 147–151
   characters and imagery, 148
   common reference points, 148
   conflict/vulnerability/achievement, 148
   moral or purpose, 147–148
   order of story, 149–151
   pacing, 148–149
   personal connection, 148
storytelling, 57, 60, 70

in C-Factor Challenge, 146–157
in change agent charisma, 125
disclosure level, 151–153
in employee charisma, 100, 101
in entrepreneur charisma, 93, 95
in family charisma, 115
in leader charisma, 75, 76–77, 81–82, 84–85, 93
list of story ideas, 153–154
in lover charisma, 106
practice in, 157
story journals, 146–147
story structure, 147–151
voice work, 154–157
styles of charisma. *see* charismatic styles
sympathetic disagreement, 166

T

Tannenbaum, Melanie, 15n
team approach
    employee charisma, 97–100
    family charisma, 112
Teresa, Mother, 8
three-part lists, 58–59, 60
Time magazine, 72

Top 2% (audio program), xi, 127
Total Voice, 155
Tracy, Brian, 14–15, 140–141, 141n
transformational leadership
    charismatic leadership *versus*, 124
    nature of, 123–124
Tumblr, 22
Twitter, 22, 54

U

unethical charisma, 18–20
    ethical charisma *versus*, 19–20
    nature of, 18–19
    preventing change, 20–21
uni-focus decision makers, 27–29
    maximizers, 28–29, 36
    satisficers, 28–29, 31, 36
University of Missouri, 112
U.S. Census Bureau, 104
Utah Jazz, 39–42

V

values
    clarifying, 139–141
    communicating, 59, 60
    in family charisma, 113, 114

Vine, 22
Virgin Group, 89–93
visibility, 163
visionary charisma, 10
   belief in, 37
   of integrative/maximizer multi-focus decision makers, 29, 31, 36
   lover charisma, 108
voice work, 154–157
   animation, 42–43
   breathing, 155
   hydration, 156
   pacing, 154–155
   pitch, 154, 156
   posture, 155, 162
   slowing down, 154–155
   yelling, avoiding, 156–157
vulnerability, in story structure, 148

W

Waldman, David A., 37–38, 37*n*
walking, 44
warmth, in kindness charisma, 37
Washington Post, The, 17–19, 72–76
water, drinking, 156
weaknesses, admitting, 88, 92
Weber, Max, 61–62
What Every Body Is Saying (Navarro), 44–51, 158–163
Winfrey, Oprah, 5, 164
Woolcott, Michael, 15–17
word choice, 87–88

Y

yelling, avoiding, 156–157
YouTube, 22
Yukl, G. A., 62